Heroines of World War II

Born in Morecambe, Lancashire, Eric Taylor served as a wartime infantry officer in North Africa and Italy. He was for many years an RAF Squadron Leader in Germany. A graduate of Manchester University, he has written several books on the Second World War including *Operation Millennium: 'Bomber' Harris's Raid on Cologne*, *Women Who Went to War, 1938–46*, *Forces Sweethearts* and *Showbiz at War*. Eric Taylor lives in York.

Heroines of World War II

ERIC TAYLOR

ROBERT HALE · LONDON

© *Eric Taylor 1991*
First published in Great Britain 1991
This paperback edition 1995

ISBN 0 7090 5768 7

Robert Hale Limited
Clerkenwell House
Clerkenwell Green
London EC1R 0HT

The right of Eric Taylor to be identified as
author of this work has been asserted by him
in accordance with the Copyright, Designs and
Patents Act 1988.

2 4 6 8 10 9 7 5 3 1

Photoset in North Wales by
Derek Doyle & Associates, Mold, Clwyd.
Printed in Great Britain by
St Edmundsbury Press, Bury St Edmunds, Suffolk.
Bound by Hunter & Foulis Ltd.

Contents

Illustrations

PICTURE CREDITS

Denis Turner: 6–7. Eveline Cardwell's family: 10–12. Nurses and staff of Coventry and Warwickshire Hospital, especially Edna Viner: 14–21. Odhams Press: 22. Australian War Memorial, Canberra: 23. Ministry of Defence Library: 24–5. Valieri and Margaret Stavridi: 26–30. American Army Signals Corps: 31–2, 34. Claire Phillips Binfords and Mort, Portland, Oregon, USA: 33. *Coventry Evening News*: 35. George Scott: 36–8. Pearl Witherington Cornioley, Paris: 39.

The author would like to thank all those who have supplied him with illustrations. All other photographs are taken from the author's own collection.

Acknowledgements

I wish to express my sincere thanks to all those people who have so generously given their time to help me with this book. In particular, my warmest thanks go to Air Commodore Dame Felicity Hill for her ideas and encouragement, to Group Captain Ian Madelin of the Air Historical Branch, Thomas Piath of the United States Army Awards Branch, Gerald Luchino of the Institute of Heraldry, US Army, Mary Wilkinson and Mark Seaman of the Imperial War Museum, and Mrs Jacqueline Freckmann at the Library of Congress, Washington DC.

I am most grateful for the help given to me by staff of the Public Record Office and the British Newspaper Library and for the research facilities granted to me by the University of York.

For the details of personal experiences of heroines mentioned in this book I have benefited greatly from conversations with former Special Operations Executive agent Pearl Witherington Cornioley in Paris, and her sister Jackie Witherington. Accounts from Mrs Margaret Stavridi, Mr Valieri Stavridi, Mrs Hadjilazaro, Colonel Hamilton-Fairley and Major Tom Clarke enabled me to build up the overall picture of Joanna Stavridi's ordeal. I owe a special debt of gratitude to former nursing sisters Edna Viner, Joan Ottaway Holman, Gladys Spencer Crichton and Beti Howe. For putting me in touch with most useful contacts I should like to record my appreciation to Mrs A.H. Button (formerly Section Officer Grace Archer), Derek Stockwell, Diana James of *Reader's Digest*, Pam of Binfords and Mort in Oregon, USA, and librarian Tom Dickinson of New York.

Once again, I should like to acknowledge my gratitude to Hy Schorr for his help and research in the USA and to my friend military historian Charles Whiting for his unfailing assistance and advice.

Finally, I am indebted to my wife Sheila not only for her continuous encouragement but also for her real contribution with initial research and proof reading. Lastly and by no means least, a special thank you to Anne Milner who, as always, rose to the challenge of presenting an immaculate typescript for the publishers within a daunting time schedule.

E.T.

Author's Note

It is, in my opinion, true that women have an inner
power which enables them fearlessly to count the
cost and then pay the price.

Irene Ward, DBE, MP

Whenever the topic of Second World War heroines is raised, certain names will always spring to mind: names such as Odette Churchill (Sansom Hallowes), Daphne Pearson, Violette Szabo and Noor Inayat Khan, all awarded the George Cross. Amongst other well-known names no doubt would be that of the extraordinary Nancy Wake, known as the 'White Mouse', who consistently thumbed her nose at the Nazi SS battalions searching for her as she commanded thousands of tough French guerillas. Remembered also would be 'one of the most truly noble women of our time' – as the press later called her – Matron Helen Rodriguez, daughter of a Scottish nurse, who defused bombs single-handed, was bayoneted, starved and tortured by the Japanese, yet refused to abandon her patients in her Burma hospital.

Equally deserving of mention would be countless hitherto unsung heroines of the women's services and also the experiences of the 3,076 British nurses who lost their lives. So many women in World War II exhibited exemplary qualities of absolute dedication to duty, and endurance so determined, in face of horrifying hardships and relentless pressures, that one cannot but marvel at their infinite resources. There is, about so many of them, a touch of Joan of Arc.

It was therefore with some reluctance that in this study of heroines I deliberately avoided dealing with the better known names. As with any book of this nature, numerous stories had to be left out for lack of space. Those I have included present a harrowing picture. These tales are, in the main, blood-stirring ones which stretch the reader's credibility to the limit, but are factually true nevertheless.

None of these women had any experience of military life before the war, yet most of them knowingly put themselves at risk for lengthy periods of time despite the fact that often the soft option for self-preservation was close at hand. Deliberately they chose a course of action which completely disregarded their own safety because 'it seemed the right thing to do at the time'.

It is only right too that their contribution to Allied victory should be recorded so that future generations will know that women themselves sought no protection because of their sex when national survival was at stake. Their gallantry, in fact, epitomizes the whole spirit of the fight against Nazi tyranny.

In presenting and scrutinizing the achievements of this particular selection of heroines I have tried to look inside the women to determine what it was that made them tick. Why did they selflessly give so much in a conflict ordained and directed by men? What was it that gave them the strength, courage and determination to triumph as they did over adversities terrifying in the extreme? Questions such as these form the thread that pulls all these stories together – the thread of motivation.

From the time of Boudicca, women have been stimulated into action by the extreme peril of their country. They have gone to war and in moments of crisis have risen to the occasion with a nobility and heroism unsurpassed.

Never was this more so than in the Second World War, when women displayed that heroism which has given them an assured place in the annals of human endurance.

1

Underground Operator

If this recital horrifies you, if you would rather not be told of it, consider a moment, it was the price one woman had to pay for our freedom.

Irene Ward, DBE, MP[1]

In that beautiful but terrible summer of 1940, when the people of France woke up from the nightmare of Germany's triumphant blitzkrieg, they found themselves powerless, a defeated nation. And, gradually, as realization of their predicament dawned upon them, everyone was faced with an appalling dilemma: should they just lay down their arms and accept the new government's treaty with Germany, or should they seek freedom by continuing the fight in some way or other?

The majority of people simply became resigned to the fact that the war was lost and an armistice leading to peace was a realistic policy. As Marcel Tardieu, a young trainee journalist at the outbreak of war, explained:

I was a reluctant conscript of 1939, called up in my teens from a small village near Vierzon and I had grown up listening to stories from my parents and neighbours of how so many of the young men of the village had been lost, dying in terrible conditions of mud and blood on the Western Front as their generals threw them into one pointless attack after another in the face of fierce machine-gun fire, only to win or lose a few yards of No Man's Land. Every village had its war memorial with its pitiful bunch of flowers withering in the sunshine below a long list of dead heroes. Sometimes there would be three or four all with the same family name. We learnt too at school what all the suffering was like. Frankly I was relieved when I heard that my war had ended so soon. I don't mind admitting it, I was

13

happy to have saved my skin and be alive still with two arms, two legs and two eyes. And if some people think the armistice was shameful, well, my answer was that it was far less shameful than carrying on fighting to kill a few million more men. And another thing, when you talk about resistance you've got to remember that it was the official government of the country that had negotiated the armistice and resistance meant treason to that same French government. There were two sides to the question, which people tend to forget.

Another thing – those who dabbled in resistance groups not only put themselves at risk but also their families and neighbours.[2]

It was no easy choice.

Those who felt like Marcel Tardieu collaborated passively, but there were others who went further. They wanted to link France with Germany more positively, to break away from the weak French governments which had bedevilled the inter-war years and establish a Fascist-style nation and a single political party which would allow France once again to play a significant role in Europe, especially in the new order.

In arguing the merits of active collaboration the enthusiasts pointed to what they called the treachery of their former ally, Britain, who, they said, had denied them adequate air support and had run away from the battle by evacuating her army from Dunkirk. Their cause gained ground when Britain's navy attacked the French fleet at Mers El Kebir to prevent it falling into German hands. Lurid accounts were published, depicting how French ships were attacked without warning, how those French battleships were sunk and 'thousands of innocent French sailors drowned'. Furthermore, these same people blamed the British naval blockade for the sudden shortage of food in the shops when the real cause was the demands made by the German army of occupation.

Consequently, though it might not be agreeable for many in France today to admit it, the fact remains that the majority of French people in 1940 were content to collaborate with the Germans. Professor M.R.D. Foot, a historian specializing in French Resistance, explained:

Collaboration was positively popular in France early in the occupation at any rate. France sent a brigade to fight with the Germans in the USSR, three thousand Frenchmen volunteered for SS divisions and there was a host of other collaborationist parties. One of these was exceptionally nasty. This was the 'Milice Francais'.[3]

It was a strong force of 10,000 regulars and 80,000 auxiliaries. Units of this black-bereted paramilitary police force imposed their own brand of terror upon members of the Resistance and Jews. By operating mainly in their own districts they had a network of informers and had a tremendous advantage over Resistance groups in that strangers or oddities could quickly be spotted and denounced. The brutality and fanaticism of this force equalled the worst of the SS Gestapo units. As 54-year-old French lawyer, Serge Klarsfield, whose father died at Auschwitz, says today: 'When you walk through French streets there are blue plaques which say "Jacques Dupont was shot on this spot by the Germans", but it never says that Dupont was first arrested by French police.'[4]

It was into such hazardous waters that women agents, trained in Britain, were plunged. It was not always easy for them to blend anonymously into a social background which could be so unreliable, apprehensive and often hostile.

Despite all the risks involved however, there were French men and women too who were prepared to fight back against the German invader. They felt ashamed and angry about the way that the leader of defeated France, Marshal Petain, had abjectly surrendered and set himself up as the symbol of collaboration. One such opponent to collaboration, Lisette Goddard, a chic silvery-haired woman in her early sixties, expressed the opinion of many who felt as she did:

> It was unthinkable to accept the armistice. After all, in 1940 we still had a large fleet and we had the colonies. There was nothing to stop the government carrying on the fight from one of these colonies. I think the surrender was appalling and so did my brother. He joined the Resistance right from the start and I stayed in the village helping in whatever way I could.[5]

Those Resistance fighters, though, needed weapons, leaders and a co-ordinating organization. They were helped by a strange collection of men and women, equally determined, from Britain.

One of these was Diana Rowden.

Squadron Officer Diana Rowden of the Women's Auxiliary Air Force was sitting one afternoon in the winter of 1940 in the chilly quiet of the RAF convalescent depot at Torquay, overlooking the blue-grey waters of Babbacombe. She was, in her tailored blue uniform, a striking young woman with rich brown hair which glinted in the pale sunshine shafting in through the windows; her hazel eyes twinkled and she had an infectious laugh. Altogether, she was in the mould of the classic beauty, with those fine features which make men's heads turn for a second look.

Her companion that afternoon, Squadron Leader William Simpson, sprawling in an armchair opposite her, had the opposite effect upon passers-by. They lowered their eyes and politely turned their heads away.

Like most of the other men in that room he did not have a real face, nor hands either. Simpson's face had been 'fried', his eyelids burnt off along with the wing of one nostril; his mouth, cheeks and forehead were ribbed with red scar tissue and his hands were ugly lumps.[6]

Around him in the sitting room were other patients like him, making 'sorties', as they called them, as if it were a flying operation, into the outside world in between surgical operations to rebuild their mutilated bodies, bodies that would never again be quite whole. Surgeons had realized that after a certain amount of time, patients got 'hospital bound' and needed a change of scene and so they were sent to convalescent depots, more like hotels than hospitals, where they could mix with ordinary people again, patients who were recovering from ordinary illnesses such as pneumonia and simple fractures. Patients like Diana Rowden, for example, rebuilding her strength after influenza.

As she sat listening eagerly to what Bill Simpson was saying she was not conscious of his appearance; that was of secondary importance. It was what he had to offer that excited her interest. He was the man who held the key to a new future for her.

Once Bill Simpson had been a pilot but a dreadful crash in the battle for France had put paid to his fighting career in the air.

By the time he had recovered from the first of many plastic surgery operations he was anxious to get back into the war somehow. He began gradually by making a series of broadcasts on the BBC Home Service entitled 'France Fights On'. And then from such small beginnings it had been but a short step across London to the Baker Street Headquarters of the Special Operations Executive where he offered his services.[7]

This new organization had been formed to foster active resistance to the Nazis in occupied countries, or, as Churchill put it, 'to set Europe ablaze'. The object was to help bring about Germany's downfall by nurturing the seeds of revolt, by systematic sabotage, and by the disruption of communications. All these tactics were to lead eventually to the building up of circuits or groups which would be adequately armed and ready to launch decisive attacks against German army units at the critical moment when the Allied armies invaded Europe.

The SOE agents operating these circuits, or '*réseaux*' as they were called in France, were all to be volunteers. Indeed, they were sometimes disparagingly called 'mere amateurs' by the traditional Secret Service. They were ordinary men and women in so far as they sprang from ordinary walks of life. They all operated in civilian clothes and were therefore subject to the same hazards in France as would be a German civilian landing by parachute in Britain at that time. They could be interrogated, tried as spies and executed. It took little imagination to picture what the Gestapo might do to such men and women. Torture and death were inevitable.

Nevertheless, despite the hazards, the recruitment of volunteers presented no problem. Why though, one might ask, was it necessary to recruit women into SOE when there were hundreds of servicemen with linguistic ability and the right spirit to tackle such 'cloak and dagger' roles? There were many reasons.

For a start, they could move about occupied countries more freely than men. Men were suspect; why were they not at work in the booming armament factories or on the land? Women had more plausible reasons for travelling. They had the excuses of visiting ailing relatives or husbands working away from home. Furthermore, women were rarely given the rigorous questioning in the street that men had to endure, and men certainly did not have their natural talent to charm.

The logic of the recruitment of women can easily be appreciated but how did these women come to know about the new secret organization of SOE? There was no possibility of calling for volunteers through Routine Orders, as might be done for other trades.

Secretly, commanding officers were asked to keep an eye open for men and women deemed suitable and willing to undertake the unknown and unimaginable hazards of being an SOE agent.

Diana Rowden, however, had never been approached by her commanding officers. She felt frustrated in her present role and would have jumped at the opportunity had it ever been offered. Now, in that strange setting of the convalescent depot Bill Simpson presented her with such an invitation. In return, she had much to offer also.

Diana Rowden had never led a life which at all fitted her for a desk job. Nor had any of her family. At an early age she had left Britain to live with her parents on a yacht, significantly called *Sans Peur*, at St Jean in southern France. It was an idyllic life for a teenager, and Diana, in the style of Huckleberry Finn, would lie sleeping on the hot deck of the yacht with a baited fishing line tied to her big toe, dangling in the water.

Anything the boys could do she could match; she was expert with a knife at gutting fish, she could haggle with tough market women, and she could sail the boat with reckless skill. Her mother remembers her as a 'turbulent tomboy, the boon companion of her two brothers, living a beach-combing life along the Mediterranean coast, a passionate devotee of boats and fishing and the sea.'[8]

When she reached secondary school age she came back to England to a school in Morayshire. One of her contemporaries there, Elizabeth Nicholas,[9] remembers Diana as 'a rather shy, red-haired girl with pale complexion and very clear reflective eyes. She hated school and all its restrictions. She was too mature for us to understand her. We were still schoolgirls in grubby white blouses concerned with games and feuds and ha-ha jokes. She was already adult and withdrawn from our diversions; none of us, I think, ever knew her.'

One would not think the two descriptions were of the same girl, the one a turbulent tomboy beach-comber, the other a pale, reflective, withdrawn character. Yet even at school there must have been something particularly distinctive about Diana for Elizabeth Nicholas to say, years later: 'I remember her with great clarity, though we met only occasionally after she left school. Perhaps even then the seeds of courage that were to ripen in war were already in her and were unconsciously made manifest to us.'

A girl, it seems, born to be a heroine.

Whilst Diana Rowden was eagerly putting questions about SOE to Squadron Leader Bill Simpson she must have gradually realized that here was the opportunity for which she had been waiting. She desperately wanted to get back to France where her knowledge of the country and her familiarity with the language could be put to positive use in helping the Allied cause.

Could the squadron leader really give her an introduction, perhaps to someone in the French Section of the SOE organization. He could and he did.

As soon as she could get her discharge from the convalescent home, Diana made her way to a massive grey, nine-storey building not far from Westminster Abbey, the Hotel Victoria. She was accompanied in the lift by a one-armed commissionaire who knocked upon a bedroom door and introduced her to the slightly built gentleman seated within.

Apart from the deal table, the chair upon which he was sitting and another plain wooden chair, the dingy room had no other furniture. The windows were boarded up – either from bomb blast or to prevent damage – and the room was lit only by one bare electric light bulb dangling from a central rosette in the ceiling.

The man who rose from his chair, as Diana entered the room, was wearing a plain grey suit and he did not look at all like a military gentleman. In fact he was a writer of thriller novels, though he was a captain in the Buffs – Selwyn Jepson. Now, like Dennis Wheatley and several other writers, he had been seconded to the Directorate of Military Intelligence.

His job was to interview and assess the potential of volunteers offering themselves for employment with the Special Operations Executive. To all those he considered acceptable for training he would give a brief explanation of the type of work upon which they might be employed and he would stress the extreme danger into which they would be putting themselves, if captured by the Gestapo. They would be operating in civilian clothes and not uniform, thereby having no protection under the International Law of Warfare. In other words, they might never return.

The risks from the Gestapo were clearly presented, but not all the other dangers. Diana would not be told that she was entering a dreadful world, a cesspit of treachery, with so much double dealing by the French, the Free French Section of SOE, and the British Secret Intelligence Service, that no one knew for certain where the truth might lie.

Small wonder agents were constantly in danger. They were tracked and harassed not only by the German Gestapo but also by the Vichy police, the Group Mobile, and Darnand's Milice. The situation was made even more difficult because of the political differences between various Resistance groups working independently.

Although it must have been made quite plain to Diana Rowden and others that SOE was a highly dangerous service to be in, it is also highly unlikely that the treacherous ramifications were ever made known in the initial briefing. Hazards were presented in a cold, objective manner and were accepted by Diana and those like her, in an equally calm way, knowing that with acceptance they were accepting also the possibility of an atrocious death.

It must be mentioned here too that as well as Diana Rowden there were, by the end of the war, thirty-seven other women agents working in Nazi-occupied France and scores of other SOE agents serving in all theatres of operations: North Africa, Italy, Greece, Persia, Iraq, Egypt, Libya, Jamaica, the United States, India, Burma and Malaya, to name only those that immediately come to mind. Diana's experience serves to illustrate what life was like for those in 'Special Operations'.

The SOE agents were not in any way 'secret agents' as were spies of the Secret Intelligence Service. Once in the field, SOE agents were known by several local people and sometimes, again unlike spies, the agent's parents knew what type of work their daughter or son was engaged upon, as did Diana's mother for example, although agents were expected to tell their nearest relative merely that they worked for some ministry, like the Ministry of Economic Warfare.

Abroad, in the field, agents were expected to make no recognition of friends or colleagues they might pass in the street. The reason for this was that enemy agents might be on watch near Resistance headquarters, and follow those who were greeted as colleagues or friends. Giving nothing away was the key-stone of security.

Ideal agents, though, were rare. Those who were excessively obsessed with security got very little done beyond staying alive and remaining undetected. Those who did not pay sufficient attention to security or who were rash and fatalistic about their future, achieved much in a short time but rarely survived. Gradually agents got used to the fear and it was then that some mistakes were made.

Diana Rowden, however, recognized the importance of security drills and even during training followed the routines

meticulously. The course was rigorous and intensive. She
learnt how to operate and maintain her radio transmitter, how
to conceal documents and to pick locks. She trained in methods
of escape and evasion, in how to move across country by night,
how to destroy bridges, railways and roads using dynamite,
plastic explosives and ammonal, how to cause lasting damage
to electricity pylons and, in addition to all this technical
training she completed a fitness training course which included
the various methods of unarmed combat and silent killing.

Apart from the arts of survival and sabotage Diana had also
to learn the complex art of achieving a complete transformation
of identity and of assuming the new one naturally – as to the
manner born. A tall order indeed!

For a start, she would have to be indisputably French. She
would have to have a cover story for her background starting
right from the moment of birth and she would have to be well
versed in all the details. This meant being rehearsed at odd
times of the day and night; early in the morning – the time
when the Gestapo knocked upon the door before people were
properly awake – questions would be asked about her family,
her school, her home town. Late at night following an
exhausting physical endurance march, she would be questioned again, brutally at times, with two men acting the parts of
tough and callous Gestapo interrogators.

All this training was also part of the selection process. How
did these men and women stand up to the strain? Would they
crack? No one was playing games. Those who wilted under
training interrogation would be likely to cave in and tell secrets
if captured by the French police or German Gestapo. Everyone
was pushed to the limit of physical and mental endurance.

The superficial elements of the new identity were provided
by a woman who specialized in those matters, Vera Atkins. She
knew France well and still had many contacts there who kept
her up to date with all the latest regulations regarding travel,
food rationing, permits for work and personal identity cards.
Clothing was important, for British clothing was easily
recognizable. Vera Atkins saw to all that, providing French
cloth and French tailors' tabs. In the pockets were suitable
photographs of bogus relatives or imaginary husbands
working away in another part of France. The material reeked of
Gauloise cigarettes.

One agent, Jacqueline Nearne, took the clothes side of the
new identity so seriously that she even knitted her own socks

because she thought the enemy could distinguish between the weave of British manufactured socks and the French – she became known as Jackie Red Socks.[10]

At last Diana Rowden was deemed ready for despatch. But only those sending her to France knew that she had still much to learn about survival once she got over there, as did all those young women agents. It was so easy to give oneself away, by some small inconsequential act to betray one's identity. Colonel Maurice Buckmaster, the man at the head of the French Section of SOE, later explained:

> The kind of thing against which we were powerless to protect an agent was instinct, or actions which had become so automatic as to rank as instinctive. One of our girls landed in France in 1943 and successfully reached the large town where she was due to rendezvous with a local Resistance man. In the middle of the town she was obliged to cross a main road. As she went to cross it she looked right to check that the road was clear; this of course is the natural thing to do if the traffic drives on the left hand side of the road. Seeing the road clear, she started to cross; a howl of brakes and curses of a lorry driver revealed her mistake.[11]

Unfortunately for this young woman, as she fell back in shock upon the pavement, a small crowd gathered round. Amongst them was a Gestapo agent who had seen everything happen and with the speed of Sherlock Holmes deduced that the real reason for the girl's foolishness in stepping off right in the path of an oncoming lorry was that she was not only a stranger to those parts but also unfamiliar with the traffic code of the country. He arrested her before she could scramble to her feet.

Instinctive actions are difficult to curb. Another girl dozed off in a railway carriage which later became crowded. As she dropped into sleep she slumped sideways and her head rolled on to the shoulder of a man sitting next to her. It partially roused the young woman from her sleep and she muttered, 'Oh, I'm sorry.' She got off at the next station and the man followed her. Once she had left the station he fell into step alongside her and told her what had happened. Fortunately for the girl, this time the man was on her side, a member of the local Resistance.[12]

Such were the hazards that young Diana Rowden would have to guard against now that she was ready to return to

France. Her survival would demand a different kind of courage from that needed by soldiers on the battlefield, where companionship kept men steady. Operating in isolation, she would have to put up with the feeling of loneliness that could be almost as agonizing as fright. The strain, she had heard, would leave her nerves ragged at times; the strain of being one person and pretending to be another, the strain of keeping silent when those around her chattered away freely. But she was ready and prepared for all that.

What was it that gave this young woman the strength to tackle the tasks ahead? What was it that motivated her? Was she doing it for the thrill, the kicks? The same kind of excitement that leads the high-wire artiste and the trapeze acrobat to perform without a safety net, or the mountaineer to climb the north face of the Eiger? Who really knows? Who can accurately analyse his or her own motives?

Diana's mother had her own theory. She had known about the work for which her daughter had volunteered, and had tried to dissuade her but in the end came to the conclusion that everybody ultimately has to learn to live her own life in her own way and from her own experience. And, though filled with trepidation, Mrs Rowden stopped trying to dissuade her daughter. She felt that Diana might have been motivated by a feeling of hatred and anger about the way that Germany had violated the country to which she had grown so attached in her youth. This blend of love and fury seemed to fortify Diana's resolution to do something about it and nothing would deflect her from her purpose.

Whatever the reason, now the training was over, Diana was eager to go.

The call to go to France came on 16 June 1943. A black car with curtains all round the rear windows called for Diana in the late afternoon and drove her up the Great North Road through Hendon and Biggleswade before turning off into a small country road lined with tall hawthorn hedges. It led to the small village of Tempsford.

In the gathering dusk on that journey, Diana, peering through the curtains, must have known that she could be taking her last look at the English countryside. What thoughts would be rushing through her mind? There would still be time to change her mind.

The car left the winding road and traversed several bumpy

tracks before drawing up alongside the porch of an eighteenth-century mansion hidden amongst trees. There, Diana was met by Vera Atkins, a cheerful woman of indeterminate age, dressed in tweed skirt and jacket. She had a round pleasant face, framed by neat, shortly cut hair and she exuded competence and confidence. Immediately she took charge of Diana, who, as already instructed, was wearing her 'going away' clothes. This was an outfit made specially for her by a French seamstress. Clothes which now had the feel about them that old, well-worn clothes have, a feeling of belonging, for Diana had deliberately been wearing the newness off, living in them as actors sometimes do before taking part in historical plays, to get right into the role they have to play.

After a coffee and cigarette, the last English one for some time, Vera Atkins took Diana into a small room for the final search, as meticulous as any Gestapo officer would make, looking for tell-tale signs: the stub of a theatre ticket, flakes of Virginia tobacco in the corners of pockets, a forgotten bus ticket. When the inspection was over Vera Atkins gave Diana a handbag in which were her local identity card, ration card and French money together with a small purse of French cosmetics and toothpaste.

Briefing came next. She was to fly to the Jura, close to the Swiss frontier to the east of the Dijon–Lyons road. There she would be met by her chief, John Starr, for whom she was to act as courier. All procedures completed, there came the inevitable period for contemplation, the waiting and wondering as minutes dragged by. Even now, there was still time for second thoughts and to say 'No, I won't go.'

On a radio in the next room the news told of King George VI visiting troops in North Africa, resting after their victories over Rommel's Afrika Korps, and of the RAF and US Air Force air blitz on Sicily, Sardinia and the Italian mainland, clearly a 'softening-up' process for the imminent Allied landings in southern Europe.

Now the sky was really darkening. Soon it would be night and she would be out there alone. A car drew up noisily and the driver came in and spoke in a low voice to the RAF officer seated at a blanket-covered table. Each of them avoided looking directly at the young pale-faced woman dressed in an overall and ready for departure. For a moment or two they stood silent. Then the officer nodded and the driver walked over to Diana. It was time to go to the aircraft.

Two other women and a man then joined Diana. They were Cecily Lefort, Noor Inayat Khan and Charles Skepper. Together they drove through the trees and on to the airfield where two small aircraft, painted matt-black, stood waiting. They looked puny, fragile things, held together by string and wire. To all intents and purposes the single-handed Lysander appeared fit merely for its original purpose of army co-operation, spotting enemy troop movement and the fall of Royal Artillery shells on targets. But this Lysander was different. It had been extensively modified, fitted with the latest specially tuned Merlin XXX engine and long-range fuel tanks which gave it a range of up to 700 miles. All guns, bomb racks and non-essential equipment had been removed to provide space for passengers.

'Lizzie', as pilots called this remarkable aircraft, could touch down and take off on a level field in thirty-five yards – about the length of one and a half cricket pitches. The training of pilots and agents was so refined, especially in the drills of landing and embarkation, that the black aircraft would be vulnerable on the ground for no more than four minutes between touch-down and take-off. Indeed, Lizzie was an ideal aircraft for sneaking across the Channel into France to deliver and pick up agents.

The Lysander pilot helped Diana into the cramped space of the passenger seat and then climbed into his own. He looked at his watch. From far away across the airfield the controller's lamp flashed green. The Lysander's engine revved twice and its nose headed into the wind. Slowly then it moved forward, engine racing to a screaming pitch as though in protest at the effort being asked of it, then it lifted upwards and headed south towards France.

They crossed the Channel at 4,000 feet. At the French coast three or four searchlights groped for the plane and then gave up, for the Lysander now had dropped right down to 400 feet. At that height, German anti-aircraft defences were ineffective.

Cruising now at about 185 miles an hour, the pilot was navigating by the light of the full moon, peering down at the landmarks of spires and rivers, checking occasionally the map on his knee, verifying his position as the black shadow of his wing fled across the pale fields below. Absolute navigational accuracy was essential and without a navigator this threw a tremendous responsibility on the pilot trying to find a tiny field that would be lit by three feeble torch batteries whilst all around the moonlit sky bristled with menace. Everything depended upon the man now flying with the map on his knee. The lives of many brave Resistance fighters were at stake. Few of them knew how fine was the dividing line between success and failure.

Soon Diana began to shiver, feeling the cold beneath her thin overall which was covering clothes meant for a French summer. They were now approaching Tours and the pilot switched on his ultra-short wave wireless set and listened for the direction signal. He dropped lower to 3,000 feet, searching in the waning moonlight for the markers. Then, at the same moment Diana and the pilot saw it, a flashing pinpoint of light far over to the left: the agreed letter 'G'. As they flew closer they spotted the three torch lights in the shape of an inverted 'L'. They were in the centre of a frighteningly tiny field bordered by trees and hedges. The Lysander swooped down, its landing gear touched and then bounced off the rough surface, then it was bumping along, curving round to its take-off position. The other Lysander followed seconds later.

The canopy slid back. Diana jumped out, clutching her cheap French fibre suitcase and handbag, and was quickly followed by her colleagues. There was a short 'OK', a roar of the engine and the two aircraft were bouncing away once more, winging their way into the night.

Diana stood there with the others for a moment or two sucking in the night air, every muscle quivering. She was back in her beloved France. Back but doomed.

Dark figures ran towards them, men with round berets pulled low on their heads, Remy Clement and his reception party. One of them gripped Diana's arm, established her identity and quickly guided her over the rough meadow to a narrow path through a small copse and on to a metalled country road. Moonlight was giving way to dawn as they hurried along, panting, their shoes seeming to clatter noisily in the misty stillness. For ten minutes, running and walking, then running again alternately, they made their way. Then, suddenly the man stopped, took a deep breath and walked Diana forward in the purposeful but less hurried gait of two ordinary people on their way to work.

A building loomed ahead. Diana recognized it from her briefing – the small town railway station. On the platform two or three red lights glowed as workmen pulled hard on their Gauloise cigarettes.

Diana's guide went to the ticket office, then he took her arm again and walked her slowly down the platform. There they stood, still and silent. Waiting. Not by any movement nor by any sound drawing attention to themselves. At last, an ancient clanking steam train drew up, workmen hovering nearby groped for door-handles. Diana's guide helped her forward and into a smoky, dimly lit carriage and then with barely a grunt of goodbye turned and made off into the mist of the dawn. His part in the story was over.

Now Diana was on her own.

It was a terrible feeling. A moment of truth if there ever was one. There she was in a foreign country, not even a part of the country she had known before. She felt utterly vulnerable. Deliberately she set about trying to calm her nerves. She began to run through her cover story. How did it begin? Had she learnt it well enough? She had thought she knew it backwards but …? Under questioning at this hour of the morning when all she wanted was the comfort of a cup of tea and the reassurance of a friendly face, how would she respond?

She looked around her in the darkened train. Men moved along the corridor and she saw the dark hand of the enemy wherever she looked. There was much she did not know. Were her identity papers good enough? Did her clothing look all right?

Fortunately for her then she did not know the reality of her situation or she would surely have been gripped by a petrifying fear.

The reality was that the Acrobat Resistance circuit she was about to join was already crumbling. The organization had been betrayed. Arrests were being made that dawn; German SD (Sicherheits Dienst Security) agents were even then on her tail, travelling with her. At small village railway stations on the 280-mile journey east to the Jura, men got out of the carriage and others got in and, with an almost imperceptible nod, handed Diana over to the next surveillance team.

Eventually the train drew in to Diana's small station, St Amour, in the Jura mountains, midway between Lyons and Besançon, scarcely forty miles from neutral Switzerland. She had been told that there the Resistance movement was very strong; she would be among friends. Her job as a courier under her code name of Paulette, would be to help in the co-ordination of their activities and the parachute drops of arms and ammunition.

Within an hour of her arrival at the station she was with her immediate chief, Captain John Starr, and the next morning she was busy at the work for which she had trained. She settled in remarkably quickly and it seemed as though she was going to be a great help to Starr and the whole Acrobat circuit. Everything was going smoothly and according to plan. But whose plan?

What Diana did not know was that her group was already so deeply compromised by treachery that although some sabotage was being carried out, the days of those saboteurs was numbered. For the moment, however, it suited the German security service to bide its time on the grounds that a known agent is a much better thing than an unknown agent as far as counter-espionage surveillance is concerned. The known agent can be monitored, followed and his contacts noted until a much larger group can be penetrated and eventually arrested. The fact that a railway junction might be blown or part of a factory destroyed mattered little in comparison with the possibility of taking out the core of a sizeable network.

Thus Diana was left free to perform her work whilst being kept under close observation.

Naturally she was completely unaware of her perilous situation or perhaps she would not have been quite so exceptionally active during those last weeks of June and early July. Her duties as co-ordinating courier took her to Lyons, Marseilles, Besançon, Montbeliard and even as far north as Paris. Frequently she would be out at night with the local French Resistance leader, the burly Monsieur Clerc, supervising at the parachute-dropping zones the delivery of arms, ammunition and explosives, which she and her wireless operator, Gabriel, had arranged.

'She was absolutely without fear,' recalled Monsieur Clerc.[13] And it was with one of those deliveries of explosives that Diana and Monsieur Clerc brought off a remarkable and new form of sabotage: sabotage by consent.

One evening the pair of them, Diana and Monsieur Clerc, called upon a senior member of the Peugeot family at Souchaux. There a branch of the well-known French car manufacturers had a factory which had been taken over by the Germans and turned into an assembly line for tank turrets, for the German army.

Diana and Monsieur Clerc offered Peugeot a choice. He

could have his machinery in the factory carefully and selectively blown up without damaging the fabric of the building or he could have the whole complex – the factory and surrounding residential area – plastered by bombs from the Royal Air Force. Peugeot opted for the selective destruction. Peugeot's staff co-operated clandestinely with the Acrobat Resistance group and, in the middle of August 1943, witnessed a terrific explosion in the factory which shattered all the vital machinery. No more tank turrets came from Peugeot at Souchaux.

Buoyed up by this success and by the increasing deliveries of arms and ammunition via the parachute drops which Diana arranged, the Resistance groups in the Jura attracted more and more recruits. Soon the nearby Maquis, hitherto regarded by German military commanders disparagingly as mere bandits, became so well armed and organized they formed themselves into the 159th Regiment of Infantry. Again, Diana played a major role in this development. As Monsieur Clerc would later testify, Diana 'helped to get us arms when we were in hiding, she helped to build our morale and the 159th Regiment owed so much to her.'[14]

Today it hardly seems credible that such a young woman with so little previous military experience should exert such a great influence on events. It was that 159th Regiment which, months later, liberated the whole region from the German yoke. By then, however, Diana was heading directly towards the execution chamber, her Acrobat circuit completely destroyed.

The first blow to the Acrobat circuit fell on Diana's chief, John Starr. A traitor called Martin denounced him to the Gestapo. Starr was arrested, tried to escape, was shot and badly wounded and was sent to prison in Dijon. Martin, incidentally, received his reward when reading the paper some days later in a nearby *estaminet*: an SOE agent shot him through the head. Diana and her wireless operator, Gabriel, managed to escape and went into hiding; Gabriel to a saw-mill in Clairvaux and Diana to a remote hamlet at Epy.

Both Gabriel and Diana lay low for three weeks and managed to transmit the news of Starr's capture to London's Baker Street SOE Headquarters which responded by instructing them to move south to Lons-le-Saunier and begin operating again under a newly arrived SOE agent, Harry Ree.

One can imagine the feelings of Diana then. Here she was,

comparatively safe at Epy, hidden in the rolling hills leading to the majestic mountains forming the frontier of Switzerland. How often, one might wonder, did she think of the sanctuary that lay just over those hills in neutral Switzerland? There men and women were living normal lives, untroubled by fears and suspicions. There Diana could have taken refuge and slept peacefully in her bed at night. No one would have blamed her had she made for that sanctuary once her chief had been arrested. But she never countenanced this possibility. That took real courage. Anger again fortified her resolution. She detested the presence of Germans in her beloved France and the very fact of being able to work actively against them gave some release to her pent-up feelings. She knew what she had to do and was determined to do it.

It was indeed vitally important now for liaison to be maintained between the strong Resistance groups in the Jura. So Diana moved to a saw-mill near Lons-le-Saunier and started to act as courier again; for a short time it began to look as though the new *réseau*, under Harry Ree, would survive the arrest of John Starr.

There in the saw-mill she settled into a steady routine, acting the part of a working-class French girl, living in with the Janier-Dubray family, helping with the children, the cooking and the cleaning. At times however, she would disappear for days at a time. No one ever asked questions. It was from one of these journeys that she came back one day with news. Another new agent was shortly to arrive from London. She looked forward to his arrival, so did Gabriel, for the new agent would undoubtedly bring news of both their families, personal letters perhaps, and of course the very latest war news. Eagerly they awaited his arrival.

It was at about 7.30 on a bright August morning not many days later when the Janier-Dubray family were just finishing breakfast that they noticed a stranger walking purposefully down the road. Without any hesitation he made straight for their house. He knocked at the door, introduced himself as Monsieur Benoit and presented his credentials which included a letter for Gabriel from his wife. Thus he established himself as the new SOE agent just out from London.

There was, however, something about this stranger that made Gabriel uneasy, despite the letter, which undoubtedly was from his wife. He became all the more anxious when, shortly after his arrival at the saw-mill house, Benoit said that he had to return to the nearby town of Lons-le-Saunier in order to pick up a suitcase which he had left there. Off he went but Gabriel, uncharacteristically, stayed inside the house all day, so uneasy was he. Diana, however, was not disturbed and she went out later, also to Lons-le-Saunier.

Early that evening when Madame was cooking dinner and Gabriel was playing chess, Diana and Benoit walked in together. For a few minutes they all chatted amicably until suddenly the kitchen door crashed open and German soldiers burst in, menacing everyone with machine pistols. Outside, cars of the Feldgendarmerie screeched to a halt and more police surrounded the house.

Diana was trapped. Her hands were manacled and along with Gabriel and Benoit, also manacled, she was hustled away to prison.

Just before midnight that same evening, the Janier-Dubray family had a surprising visitor – Benoit. He walked into the house freely, on his own, and demanded the wireless transmitter. This Benoit was not the real Benoit at all! He was an impersonator. The real Benoit, like many other victims of the double dealing, had been met by a German reception committee. Possibly shaken and demoralized by what had happened, the real Benoit might have provided whatever was asked of him by the Germans and his place was taken by a treacherous Frenchman working for the German Gestapo. Having satisfied himself by his early morning visit of the whereabouts of Diana and Gabriel, he had later led the German Field Security police to the saw-mill.

The most terrible time of all now began for Diana. First she was taken to the dreaded headquarters of the Gestapo at 84 Avenue Foch in Paris. Neighbours in the elegant adjoining houses talked in whispers about screams coming late at night from the top floor of the innocent-looking five-storey house. There it was that specially trained interrogators practised their art of pulling out toe nails or dribbling water down a victim's nostrils as he was tilted back in a chair, until his lungs slowly filled with water.

Diana was incarcerated in a bare, cell-like room immediately below the roof in what, before the war, had been the maid's room. A little air and light came in through a large sky-light that opened on to the roof, but there was no possibility of escape that way. The sky-light frame was sealed off by strong iron bars bolted on to metal pieces attached to the rafters. To that room came Diana's interrogators at odd times of day and by night. They tried to convince Diana that they already had a wealth of information and that whatever else Diana knew was really of little consequence, so she might as well save herself a lot of pain and trouble by talking freely. Diana, though, had been well schooled in these techniques and maintained a stony silence which infuriated her interrogators. Eventually they appeared to give up and despatched the stubborn English woman to Fresnes prison just outside Paris where they hoped to undermine her resistance by long-term psychological treatment.

Fresnes prison stands in a valley on a minor road south of Paris where mist gathers and damp creeps up the masonry. Every day there, in damp cells, obscenities were inflicted upon men and women existing on the most meagre of diets. Shortly after dawn, the routine started with shouts of *'raus', 'raus'*, the stamp of heavy boots upon concrete, the rumbling of the food trolley bringing thin ersatz coffee known by everyone as 'acorn juice', a few grammes of bread and the occasional fatty sausage. The noise never stopped – the click-clack of cell doors, the rattling of chains and the slamming of peep-hole covers. Prisoners roused themselves for a day of recurrent cravings for food, for hours in which they thought of all the meals, the drinks and the cigarettes they had previously taken for granted.

Now, in addition to being deprived of everything to which they had been accustomed, they could never pass more than an hour each night without being wakened by the guard slamming the metal peep-hole, flashing a light upon them to make sure they were still alive, and then slamming the slot cover back again.

Often, in the dark hour before dawn, the knell would toll for the hostages – those about to be executed in reprisal for the murder of German soldiers by civilians and acts of sabotage. This brought cries and screams of revolt bordering on madness from the innocent condemned who were being led away to their deaths.

At this time too, SS guards would charge along the corridors flinging open doors and ordering inmates to dress for 'Tribunal'. Diana would listen to the steps nearing her cell, wondering if they would pass her door, but all too often the 'Tribunal' call was for her. Then Diana would be driven through the Paris streets in the *'panier à slade'*, a Black Maria into which prisoners were rammed in tiny cubicles of wire mesh on each side of the truck. The lucky ones could look through the iron grill of the rear door and see men and women sipping drinks on pavement cafés accompanied by German officers enjoying the bright sunshine. Life for most people was going on as pleasurably as usual. For women like Diana who would not co-operate, life had nothing to offer but pain and, inevitably, a lonely, terrifying death.

Visits to Gestapo Headquarters for 'Tribunal' usually followed a fixed routine: three hours locked in a room with no contact whatsoever, then, occasionally a delicious hot meal of meat and potatoes. This was quickly followed by a move to another office where a pleasant young man might offer a cigarette and ask innocent questions about names, dates of birth, names of parents, sisters, brothers, schools attended and so on until a fluency of replies had been established. The easy flow of answers would lead to more vital questions such as the names of officers commanding neighbouring Resistance groups. For those who answered in the rehearsed training school pattern of 'I have nothing to say', there would be further visits conducted by men with cold eyes and impassive faces, hand-picked efficient young men who had graduated from Heinrich Himmler's school, men who knew how to make people talk. Men who could inflict pain and still excuse their bestiality by claiming it was no more cruel than that inflicted by RAF aircrew dropping bombs on women and children in German cities.

It was after several painful visits to 84 Avenue Foch that Diana found herself there one afternoon for the last time and in unusual company. Crammed into the same room with her were six other women who, after a few minutes together, gradually realized that they were all British SOE agents. A decision had been made. It was May 1944: time for such prisoners to be moved from France to Germany. The Allied invasion was imminent. These women knew too much. Collectively they would be able to point a finger at traitors. They could not be allowed to fall into Allied hands.

So it was that on 12 May 1944 these seven women were manacled and marched out between ranks of a heavily armed SS platoon to the transport taking them to the Paris Gare de L'Est. There, Diana Rowden, Madeleine Damerment and Elaine Plewman were put into one compartment and the other four women, Yolande Beekman, Andree Borrel, Vera Leigh and

Odette Sansom were packed into the adjacent one with SS guards. At 6.30 that evening the train pulled out of Paris and slowly jolted its way across France, over the Rhine and then, with frequent long halts due to RAF bombing raids, into the heart of Germany.

At Karlsruhe the seven women left the train and were driven in taxis through the city in which people looked well clothed and well fed on the plunder from occupied countries, to the women's prison in Riefstahlstrasse. Another terrifying routine began, for these women had a label of 'special prisoners', deserving strictest surveillance. They were classified as 'NN' – women bound for the '*Nacht und Nebel*', the night and the fog in which they were to disappear without trace.

The arrival of the women disrupted the regular routine of the prison and the governor did not like it. He informed Gestapo Headquarters in Berlin that he had no facilities for guarding such political prisoners and asked for special instructions as to their supervision. These instructions eventually arrived; the women were to be given 'special treatment', the cryptic euphemism for execution.

So it was that at four o'clock on the morning of 6 July, Diana Rowden, Vera Leigh and Andree Borrel were woken and told to get ready for a move. They were to go to another camp 'for agricultural work'. Whilst they were waiting for transport they were joined by a fourth SOE woman, Sonia Olschanesky.

At about three o'clock that same day, Brian Stonehouse,[15] an SOE agent imprisoned in the all-male Natzweiler concentration camp, was digging a ditch near the perimeter fence when a fellow prisoner tapped him on the shoulder and pointed towards an unusual spectacle. Approaching them down the path were four women in civilian clothes with two SS guards. The women were each carrying various parcels; one of them had a cheap fur coat over her arm. Stonehouse recalled later that all these women seemed to be in their early twenties and looking white and weary. They passed close to the working party and he could study them closely.

By the time the prisoners had finished their digging and returned to their huts a rumour was already going around that these women were English. Then another strange thing happened. The loudspeakers blared forth a warning that all prisoners were to be confined to their huts at eight o'clock, they were to put up the black-out boards and not to show their faces at any window at the risk of being shot for failure to comply.

Clearly some sinister business was afoot.

The grim story of what really happened next was pieced together by Squadron Officer Vera Atkins who had originally helped to despatch these agents from Britain to France and consequently felt some responsibility for them as well as to their relatives. She was determined to discover the truth of their fate and bring those responsible to justice. She did just that. After the war the SS murderers were quickly brought to trial at Wuppertal in May/June 1946. Then it was that the barbaric details emerged of how those four heroic young women were sent to an awful death.

At first the accused staff of Natzweiler charged with atrocities had little to say, but as soon as one or two of them, believing themselves to be merely innocent minions obeying orders, began to talk, then the principal protagonists in the macabre affair opened up too and talked dispassionately of what they had done on orders from higher command. Soon they were all talking at length, seeking to incriminate both their subordinates and seniors in order to save their own skins. Consequently, from all the evidence at the trial and from the statements from men who survived Natzweiler concentration camp, the horrific sequence of events leading to the deaths of these four women could be fairly accurately reconstructed.[16]

It appears that when the camp commandant, Hartjenstein, received from Berlin his orders to execute the women, he called for the camp medical officer, Dr Rohde, and together they discussed what would be the quickest and most humane way of dealing with the problem. Not once did they make enquiries about whether the women had been properly tried in a court of law nor did they question the legality of the sentence. It was just a tedious job that had been thrust upon them. Finally, Hartjenstein and Dr Rohde agreed to get the task over and done with right away by giving each of the women an injection of phenol and burning the bodies immediately afterwards. All trace of them would then have disappeared, as requested, into the 'night and the fog'.

Later that evening, when it was dark, SOE agent Pat O'Leary, a prisoner at Natzweiler, was looking out of the window when he saw the SS camp medical officer, Dr Rohde, marching briskly down the central pathway between the huts in the direction of the crematorium. A few minutes later, one at a time, Diana and her three comrades were led down to the crematorium for an injection. When one of the women asked what it was for, she was told, so an orderly was later to state, that it was a routine precaution against typhus. It was, instead, probably a lethal injection of phenol which produces a fairly quick, though by no means a painless, death. Immediately each woman collapsed she was taken along the corridor to the crematorium. The oven door was opened – the flash of flame spurting from the chimney into the dark night sky was seen by prisoners – and the woman was pushed inside. Another witness at the trial, Berg, claimed he had heard screams as if one woman had recovered consciousness at the moment of being thrust inside the oven. Other evidence points to the fact that one of those unfortunate women reached up and scratched the face of her executioner, Peter Straub. Those scratches would soon put a noose round his neck.

Such was the end for Diana Rowden who gave so much, so freely. Such was the price she paid for our freedom and a posthumous Croix de Guerre.

2

The Home Front Heroine

Courage is resistance to fear, mastery of fear, not
absence of fear.

Mark Twain

On 8 July 1940, Eveline Cardwell, the slim wife of a Yorkshire
farmer, made headline news as the first civilian heroine of the
Second World War.[1] A mere month later, King George VI and
Queen Elizabeth came up to Hornsea to present her with the
British Empire Medal 'for her pluck and presence of mind' in a
hazardous situation.

When all this was reported in the national press, readers
were naturally puzzled by the headlines. What on earth could
have happened in that remote part of Britain to merit an award
of such distinction? One might even wonder the same today.
The events, however, have to be seen in the context of those
dark days of the Second World War shortly after the British
Army's disastrous defeat in France and its evacuation from the
beaches at Dunkirk. It was a time when the top admirals,
generals and air marshals were meeting secretly in another part
of Yorkshire – at the Station Hotel, York – to discuss whether
Britain now had any chance at all of surviving.

Behind the hotel's locked doors and grey-yellow walls, well
away from the prying eyes of London, the Secretary of State for
War, Anthony Eden, heard the Vice Chief of the Imperial
General Staff say that in his considered opinion the British
Army was demoralized ... 'and may not be ready when the
time comes'.[2] The top brass all agreed that morale was
definitely shaky and there was no telling what the conscript
army might do if the Germans invaded.

The civilian population of Britain was worried too. The
events of May 1940 onwards had brought the Second World
War frighteningly close to home. People had followed closely

the events from dawn on 10 May when a newly equipped German army, deploying some ninety divisions and half as many again in reserve, had attacked on the Western Front with a massive air support of 4,000 planes. Hitler, ignoring Dutch and Belgian neutrality, had won swift victories: Holland gave up fighting in five days and Belgium in a fortnight. By 26 May, little more than fourteen days after Hitler's offensive began, the British Expeditionary Force was withdrawing to the coast of Dunkirk. That news was alarming.

Worse was to come when, over BBC radio, people in Britain heard emergency appeals for ships of all sizes to assemble to rescue the British and French armies from their perilous position. More than eight hundred ships responded and in one of the most dramatic operations of the Second World War, they delivered 338,000 troops safely into Britain to fight another day.

Now men and women who had grumbled about the black-out, rationing and shortened tea breaks in factories, were suddenly made aware that there really was a war on and that there was a threat to their very existence. The Prime Minister had warned the nation to 'prepare themselves for hard and heavy tidings'. Now they had come and the question was could the nation take them, or would it crack under the strain like France and the Low Countries?

Morale was of vital importance. Newspapers tried to boost it by reporting the 'Miracle of Dunkirk' and presenting the operation as a kind of victory, but few readers were deceived by such attempts at morale-boosting as the *Daily Mirror*'s headline: 'BLOODY MARVELLOUS' and by reports that 'the army had returned home with their tails up ready to have another crack at the Nazis.' The facts spoke for themselves. The British army had been chased out of France and now Britain was surely next in line for invasion.

The government feared that morale might crumble in Britain as dramatically as on the Continent and with invasion expected at any minute the nation's fighting spirit was crucial to any successful defence. Indeed, those senior officers of the three services meeting in York summed up the situation in the gravest terms: 'Our conclusion is that Germany has all the cards, but the real test is whether the morale of our fighting personnel and civilian population will counterbalance the numerical advantages which Germany enjoys.'[3]

Something would have to be done about that morale, for Lord Clark reported that it was much lower than anyone had ever dared to say. This evidence had come from government informers who questioned the public. These informers posed as members of a Mass Observation team, but were in fact secret investigators paid from Secret Service funds to prevent the public from knowing they were being spied upon.[4]

On 22 May 1940 a Home Morale Emergency Committee was set up for the purpose of suggesting measures to counter the 'dangers of a break in morale'. The Ministry of Information was now scratching round for ideas. Ministers urged the government to 'tell the War Office to provide plenty of bands and marching soldiers' and on 17 June a paper stated: 'For want of something better we shall have to plug (1) the Navy (2) the Empire's strength and (3) what a hell of a fine race we are!'

A suggestion by a Member of Parliament, E.C. Cobb, gives some idea of the degree of desperation felt about morale then. In a crowded House of Commons he stood up and put forward a proposition that 'the government should arrange for some speaker who would appeal to the masses such as a Preston North End footballer or some similar hero!'[5] (In those days Preston North End was a great First Division football club.)

Meanwhile, the Service chiefs were preparing for a massive assault from the air and as early as 5 May, Churchill had written to President Roosevelt, saying: 'We expect to be attacked here both from the air by bombing and by parachute troops in the near future.'

Warnings of the imminent possibility of German parachutists landing were included in the news bulletins on the radio of 16 May; guards were placed outside Broadcasting House and Whitehall ministries, ready to repel any attempts by parachutists to seize key points.

Rumour ran rife: corpses in field grey uniform and badly burnt bodies had been washed up on the east coast, the sea had been set on fire from submerged oil drums which ignited the moment German assault boats approached the shore, German parachutists dressed as nuns had been dropped to organize the Fifth Column of Nazi supporters amongst the British Fascists. Or so people said. Absurd though it might now seem, the BBC, broadcasting in German to Germany, warned listeners that parachutists descending in Britain dressed in anything other than conventional German uniforms would be shot out of hand. (A point Germany remembered when British women agents were later dropping in France and other occupied countries.)

On 28 May, the Minister for War, Sir Edward Grigg, told the House of Commons that 'imminent peril may descend from the skies at any moment.' Further precautions were needed.

Orders were given for all signposts throughout Britain to be taken down, all milestones uprooted and all names of villages and railway stations obliterated or removed completely.

Gangs of Irish navvies hastily erected concrete pill-boxes along the coast and road-blocks on roads approaching towns. The road-blocks were manned by trigger-happy Local Defence Volunteers whose brief was to stop cars for identification. Drivers who did not stop were shot. Four motorists were shot dead in four separate incidents on the night of 2 June. Such was the fear, bordering on panic, of invasion by parachutists.[6]

The government had forbidden the ringing of church bells, which were to be used only as a warning that invasion had begun. It even became an offence to leave a car unattended without immobilizing it by removing the rotar arm.

Alarming and confusing reports came from various government departments too. The Air Ministry produced a memorandum saying that: 'Information from Norway shows that German parachute troops when descending hold their arms above their heads as if surrendering. The parachutist however holds a grenade in each hand. These are thrown at anyone attempting to obstruct the landing.'

The inner feeling of danger was present in even the remotest areas. Hornsea, in Yorkshire's East Riding, was a forgotten little place. It had no industry. Fishing had died out years before and by 1940 the day tripper had vanished. Hornsea, they quipped, was a place you came to to die. Yet Hornsea too was aware of the new threat from over the 'German Ocean', as its old retired inhabitants still called the North Sea.

At mid-day on 8 July 1940, a 45-year-old Hornsea farmer's wife, Eveline Cardwell, was listening to the BBC news when a farm hand burst into her sitting room, panting for breath. He stood there for a moment as if suddenly aware of the muddy mess his boots had made on the master's carpet, and then began to stutter, 'Them paratroops ... they're landing on our fields!'

One can imagine the feeling of this woman. She was alone. Her husband, an officer in the LDV, was away on farm business, her son in the army. The immediate response of this doughty Yorkshire woman was to run to the telephone. It was dead. Had the parachutists cut the wires? She leapt into action, grabbed the farm boy and despatched him on his bike to warn the police.

She hurried then to take her husband's shotgun from the cupboard. Second thoughts made her change her mind. Reasoning that the parachutists would be far better shots than she was herself, she made for the door empty-handed. As she stood for a moment on the step she saw to her horror a parachutist land just beyond the hawthorn hedge at the front of her garden. He released his cumbersome harness and limped purposefully towards the farmhouse.

Eveline Cardwell put on her most determined look. Authoritatively and briskly she set off herself towards this intruder. 'He was a tall man, well over six foot three inches, and about twenty-five years old,' she recalled.[7] 'I walked straight up to him and told him to put his hands up. He did not understand until I made signs and then he raised his hands in the air.'

Somewhat reassured by his compliance, Eveline Cardwell made her next move. 'I pointed to the automatic pistol in his belt, and he handed it to me.' A few onlookers had now gathered to watch the most unusual sight of a middle-aged farmer's wife marching her six-foot prisoner towards the police station. But she had not gone more than a few paces before two British soldiers on a motorcycle and sidecar drew up and she handed over her prisoner.

His interrogation later revealed that he was not one of Hermann Goering's crack parachutists but an airman from a German Air Force squadron on a mission to bomb Sunderland. He had baled out over Flamborough Head when his pilot was killed and his aircraft set on fire by RAF Spitfires. Nevertheless, the press seized upon the story. Home Front heroines were hot news in those days, much sought after by Britain's propaganda machine, the Ministry of Information. The national press reported how the slim, unarmed Mrs Cardwell had captured a 6 ft 3 in parachutist and hailed her achievement as a 'true act of heroism' which would give the 'sort of boost to morale the whole country needed'. Another extract from the press of the day said: 'Mrs Cardwell showed no fear or emotion, the fury of the Hurricanes had nothing on this farmer's wife.'

Winston Churchill was reported as saying: 'The propaganda alone was worth a flotilla of destroyers.' News which bolstered morale in those days was avidly seized upon and given banner headlines on the premise that every age salutes valour and accepts it as an inspirational example, challenging everyone to live up to the same standards. Heroines were good news, and there was little enough to counterbalance the fearful reports that had been coming in during the last few months. There is no doubt that the media had a field day with the Hornsea heroine and the response to the interest generated was in itself remarkable. Barely thirty-six hours had elapsed before Eveline Mary Cardwell was awarded the BEM and scarcely a month went by before the King and Queen came up to Hornsea to present her with the medal.

When the Queen, speaking for her husband (who was afflicted by a speech impediment), said: 'You must have been very brave,' Eveline's husband was heard to remark, *sotto voce*, 'Very brave, yes, but *bloody foolhardy.*'[8]

Mrs Cardwell's ordeal, however, was not yet over. She was now called upon to face Hugh McDermott of the British Broadcasting Corporation for a full-length interview designed for broadcasting to the United States, Britain's unofficial and somewhat reluctant supporter at that time.

What better way was there to drive home to Mr and Mrs Average American that the ordinary folk of Britain were determined to stand up to and fight against the Nazi terror? It was a message Churchill needed to get over to the American public, for although President Roosevelt was sympathetically inclined towards Britain's plight there was still a large percentage of the American population that was totally against involvement.

The problem to overcome was that Washington had already been assured by Joseph Kennedy, American ambassador in London, that Britain would inevitably suffer defeat because she had not the will to fight.

Right from his appointment to the post in London in 1937, Joseph Kennedy had associated himself with the notorious appeasers: Chamberlain, Simon, Halifax, Hoare and members of the British aristocracy with pro-German views. Incredibly he had even claimed 'credit' for saving the peace in 1938 by influencing Prime Minister Chamberlain to trust Hitler in his Munich agreement!

Kennedy, who represented a Catholic, Irish, anti-English group in America, was a convinced isolationist preaching a gospel that America should not be dragged into another war by the perfidious British.

Within days of the outbreak of war in 1939, Joseph Kennedy gathered his wife and nine children together for a farewell dinner before packing them off to the safety of their US home. At the end of the dinner, he toasted the Germans, allegedly saying they would soon thrash the British.

Such was the man whose influence on US opinion Churchill would have to overcome if he was to persuade America to come into the war. In no small way, Home Front heroines would be helping him in his task.

By this time, Churchill had the country behind him. In the grim days following Dunkirk the nation abandoned the appeasers, 'Holy Foxy Halifax' and 'Slippery Sam Hoare' and turned to Churchill, the rebel who had been out of office for years. A new spirit of defiance grew, a new hope and a surge of confidence which promoted a spectacular lift in morale. And morale, as that other successful wartime leader, Field Marshal Montgomery, was wont to say: 'is the greatest single factor in war'.[9]

In 1940 the odds were certainly stacked against Britain, standing alone against the might of the German war machine. Now all those virtues of heroism as defined by the dictionary – extraordinary bravery, firmness, fortitude and greatness of soul – were desperately needed. No wonder those women who demonstrated such virtues, the heroines, got maximum publicity. Their exploits fanned the sparks of courage and resolution which had lain dormant within the nation, and set them ablaze.

So it was with those news reports of Eveline Cardwell, the epitome of the ordinary housewife and mother who took on the parachutist landing near her home. And so it was too with all those servicewomen who, during the Battle of Britain and the blitz of British cities, displayed quite amazing feats of courage, fortitude and initiative whilst completely disregarding their own safety.

Corporal Joan Daphne Pearson was one who risked her life to save an RAF pilot from being burnt to death and became the first woman to hold the George Cross. Here was just an ordinary, low-ranking non-commissioned officer, a former office worker, who now rose to the heights of courage in a dire emergency.

She was asleep in her quarters when, at 0100 hours, she was awakened by the noise of an aircraft crashing quite close to the

WAAF quarters. Straight away, she rushed out to the scene of the crash and found that the pilot had been seriously injured, another officer killed outright and two airmen injured. Although the aircraft was burning fiercely and she knew there were bombs on board, she rendered first aid to the pilot and helped to get him clear of the wreckage by releasing his harness. When she and another airman had got him about thirty yards away from the blazing aircraft, one of its 120 lb bombs exploded. Knowing that others would follow, Daphne Pearson flung herself on top of the stunned pilot to protect him from blast and splinters. Two months later she received the country's second highest award for courage.

Ranking second only to the Victoria Cross, the George Cross is, in the words of King George VI himself, 'a mark of honour for men and women in all walks of life'. There were many like her that summer.

Another young woman, this time in the ATS, displayed similar gallantry when a Wellington bomber crashed near her ATS depot. Joan Myall and three of her colleagues ran to rescue the crew, at great danger to their lives and amazed a Home Guard lieutenant who had also rushed to the scene. Lieutenant Whitford, of a Midlands battalion, full of praise for the women, said: 'The bomber was blazing furiously, bullets were spattering around. There was a grave risk of an explosion which could have caused further casualties in the area and I called for volunteers to help me put out the flames. The ATS girls ran forward with buckets of water and they succeeded in saving the turret with its two loaded machine guns. Unfortunately the crew were found to be dead.'[10]

'We realized the danger but we just had to help,' said Lance Corporal Joan Myall of Berkhamsted modestly. The youngest of the ATS girls, not quite eighteen, Private Jackie Birrell of Fifeshire, was known as 'little tough guy' but all three young women with her that day deserved the same nickname. The other two, Eva James of Croxley Green and Joyce Middleton of Harrow Weald, recalled the scene with horror but said, 'We just had to do something. We couldn't just stand around watching.'

Wren Elizabeth Glen Booth of Leeds earned her award, says her citation, for

> outstanding bravery in helping to rescue the observer of a crashed and burning aircraft. She was on duty as an MT driver at Machrihanish, when a blazing aircraft fell near to her. She

drove to the spot and though explosions were scattering burning debris and petrol around, clambered on to the wreckage and helped to drag the observer clear. His clothes were already on fire. She attacked the flames in which he was enveloped, with her bare hands attempting to beat them out. She tore his smouldering clothes from him and then drove him at great speed for nine miles along a tortuous route to the nearest doctor. Unfortunately, despite all her efforts the airman died.

Such coolness and devotion to duty inspired the nation. And every little bit of it was needed then for Hitler had abandoned his dream of Britain surrendering and signing his shameful peace terms and now ordered his Luftwaffe Chief, General Goering, to 'prepare immediately and with great haste, for the great battle of the German air force against Britain'.

Obviously, for the German invasion to succeed, air supremacy was essential. Goering planned to achieve this by concentrating his attacks primarily on five radar stations in the south and south-east of England. Women had a significant role in operating these stations which provided a screen through which any intruder would have to fly, thereby forfeiting surprise. RAF fighters could then be airborne and ready to sweep down on to bomber formations approaching the coast. If the radar units could be destroyed then bombers would be less vulnerable and have a far better chance of getting through to their targets. Goering's plan was to knock out all these radar units and the Fighter Command stations by mid-September 1940, so that Hitler could launch his twenty-five divisions to land between Folkestone and Worthing on 21 September.

RAF defences however, proved stronger than the boastful Goering expected and he intensified his attacks. On 15 August a massive bombardment rained down on the fighter fields of south-east England – Dover, Deal, Hawkinge, Lympne, Middle Wallop, Kenley and Biggin Hill. On the next day, 600 bombers raided the fighter fields of Kenley, Croydon, Biggin Hill, Manston, West Malling, Northolt and Tangmere. But fighter bombers hit back savagely and scores of German bombers spiralled blazing down to earth.

The German Luftwaffe outnumbered the RAF in aircraft by nearly three to one during that long hot summer; wave after wave of Messerschmitt 109 fighters covering Junkers and

Heinkel bombers attacked the south of England. At the start of the battle, Britain had fewer than three thousand pilots; 547 of them would be killed in those few weeks, and more than a thousand aircraft lost.

Day after day, battles of incredible ferocity were taking place, often at a height of five or six miles, and the great conflict raged and thundered on as if there was no limit to men and aircraft. And though the main targets for the Luftwaffe bombers were the RAF radar and fighter stations, the naval shore establishment came in for a pasting too. During one such heavy raid, Wren Nina Marsh, a bonny, fair-haired eighteen-year-old, was wounded in the back and arm and though bleeding profusely made light of her injuries to give valuable help to the more seriously wounded Wrens and ratings as the bombs crashed down on and around the sick-bay shelter. She refused to give in until all the casualties had been evacuated to hospital. Only then did she have her own wounds attended to. They were so serious she was rushed to hospital. She survived – just – and for her meritorious devotion to duty, bravery and disregard for her own safety was awarded the British Empire Medal, Military Division. All she could say when visited in hospital by her friends was: 'I never gave it a thought. I was so angry, mad with rage at the beggars dropping those bombs.'

Fury can be a great motivator. Like the fighter pilots themselves, women in the thick of the battle on the ground just refused to give in; they were in the fight and were going to stay in it.

But as the battle developed the RAF was forced to use pilots who had little training and who had never fired their guns, even in practice. The strain on everybody in Fighter Command was enormous. There were so many attacks to meet and so few to do it. By mid-August the death of one experienced pilot was a greater loss to the squadron than the loss of ten Spitfires or Hurricanes. Replacement machines were available but experienced pilots could never be replaced.[11]

All this demanded terrific efforts from ground staff who looked after those pilots and their machines, whilst under heavy bombing attacks themselves. Airmen and airwomen displayed a kind of collective heroism which helped them to continue performing their duties at full operational efficiency.

Soon it became clear to everyone, WAAF and RAF, on those Fighter Command stations that a systematic German plan was in operation. After the first attack on Kenley it was Croydon's turn, and then it was West Malling that came in for a hammering. Who was to be next on Goering's schedule?

Biggin Hill soon found out. Their ordeal began with a brief encounter on 18 August, with nothing much to worry about for the raid lasted only one hour and most of the bombs landed on the neighbouring golf course, creating a few more bunkers than before. But then, during the next two weeks, the intensity of the raids increased dramatically. Systematically buildings, offices, hangars, barrack rooms were destroyed, until the commanding officer came to the conclusion that as long as the wreckage of the hangars remained standing the raids would go on, so he authorized their complete demolition by having them blown up. (He was subsequently court-martialled for his action but was exonerated.)

The day of decision in the life of Britain's most bombed Fighter Command station came on Friday 30 August 1940. It was a day in which heroines played a vital part.

Herman Goering was adopting totally new tactics. Having failed to drive the Spitfires and Hurricanes from the skies, the alternative was to wipe out their bases by even more intensive bombardment. The Battle of Britain had entered its most deadly phase.

On that Friday morning the good weather still prevailed; it was bright and sunny. Farmers were out in their fields early. They too had been on the alert for weeks now as falling aircraft exploded in their fields setting fire to the ripening corn. Visibility was good, between five and ten miles. Shortly after mid-day the WAAF were breaking off for their meal of Brown Windsor soup, fried bully beef and dehydrated potatoes, when the raucous hooting of the alarm came through the Tannoy loudspeakers. Men and women paused in their stride wondering which way to turn when the calm voice of their group captain came through to them: 'This is your station commander speaking. At any moment we may be attacked. I want all personnel except those engaged on essential services to take cover immediately.'

From offices and stores WAAFs scurried, talking excitedly, some giggling nervously, all converging on to the WAAF shelters. Rena Barron recalled: 'Cramped together in that concrete shelter we were silent, each alone with the same thoughts of "Am I really going to die?" Each of us was searching the others' faces for comfort and ensuring that we didn't, ourselves, give our fear away. Just a smile or a wink that said, "It's OK – I'm scared too, but we'll be all right – just hang on."'[12]

Newly promoted Sergeant Joan Mortimer was in the armoury when the alarm sounded. Stacked around her were tons of high explosive but she realized that her vital role was to stay with the switchboard, conveying urgent messages to the defensive gun positions around the airfield.

Joan, aged twenty-eight, was a popular girl on that airfield. She took a lot of banter in the armoury but she was admired for her readiness to help out with other duties. She had been indefatigable in shovelling and clearing away rubble after raids and her graceful, self-assured figure was to be seen after every raid hurrying across the airfield with a bundle of red flags under her arm, peering into bomb craters to look for unexploded bombs and marking those she saw with a red flag as a warning to aircraft landing. 'Goodness knows how many lives she saved by doing that,' said Section Officer Felicity Hanbury.[13]

Now she sat alone, tautly waiting. Then came a swelling roar which developed into a 'formidable endless stream of bombers, wave after wave of them as far as the eye could see. They flew into a curtain of anti-aircraft shell bursts but still they came on, remorselessly at high level. The first bombs fell and then spout after spout of smoke and flame leapt up from buildings on the camp and in the neighbouring villages of Keston and Biggin Hill. Others cratered the landing area.'

During the worst part of the bombardment, Joan Mortimer was kept busy relaying messages for the issue of ammunition. Then, at last they were gone. All seemed quiet. But before the 'All Clear' sounded Sergeant Mortimer knew there was still a vitally important job to be done before the squadron fighters returned to their base at Biggin Hill. The unexploded bombs would have to be marked. So, without waiting for the all clear siren, she dashed out on to the airfield with her bundle of red flags to mark the numerous unexploded bombs. On one occasion a delayed-action bomb exploded quite close to her but she carried on, inspiring, so reports said, the quaking airmen who had been detailed to help her.

Slowly, dazed and dusty, airmen and airwomen emerged from their shelters in a mood that was curiously gay with relief and the feeling of being spared. But underneath the chatter and joking lurked the unspoken awareness that tough though this raid had been, the next could be worse.

Lunch was eaten dry and cold, a bully-beef sandwich choked down with luke-warm water, before going back to the routine of the day.

At six o'clock that evening came the second stage of Goering's plan to wipe Biggin Hill of the face of the earth. This time they came in low, without any warning. Junkers 88s flying at less than a thousand feet. The noise was terrifying and the ground trembled as the new 1,000 lb bombs were dropped. Once again, Joan Mortimer ran to her post in the armoury. Other WAAFs raced to the airwomen's shelter, crouching there, waiting, fists clenched and fingernails biting into their skin.

Outside, huge recovery vehicles were being tossed upside down like children's toys by the blasts of the big bombs. Building after building erupted in clouds of debris and flame. Six bombs devastated the technical wing; the guard room and NAAFI canteen went the same way. Soon everything was obliterated by a great soaring curtain of smoke and dust.

Decorations came through quickly. DSOs and DFCs for the pilots, but there was also a Military Medal for Joan Mortimer, a man's medal for a woman's bravery in the face of the enemy. In addition, the citation went on to say, 'This airwoman displayed exceptional courage and coolness which had a great effect on the morale of all those with whom she came into contact.'

Fortunately, for the next few days heavy cloud covered western Europe and Goering's bombers were grounded. It was a time for rest, recovery and replacement. It was during this lull between attacks that two high-ranking WAAF officers came to Biggin Hill to see how their young airwomen were bearing up under the strain of enemy action. They gathered all who could be spared from essential duties to be addressed. The officers could hardly find enough words to express the admiration the Air Ministry felt for the fortitude being displayed by all under fire, who were managing to maintain such a high standard of morale despite the stress and physical weariness.

Before leaving to return to their own headquarters, the senior WAAF officer closed her address with a broad smile and the words: 'Well, now you know what it's like, it won't be nearly so bad next time.'

Those were not the sentiments of her listeners. The memory of what those bombs could do was all too fresh in their minds for any platitudes to assuage.

During this period too, morale was well to the forefront of

the station commander's mind. He noticed that the NAAFI manageress was showing signs of strain. He felt that she had contributed so much to the maintenance of morale that it was important that she should take some leave. He ignored her tearful pleading to be allowed to carry on and brusquely sent her packing on four days' furlough.

When the bombers returned, they took Biggin Hill by surprise. Airmen and airwomen were just leaving their messes after supper when they heard the familiar, steadily mounting roar of bombers from the south-east. There was no mistaking them – Junkers 88s – and as if to confirm everyone's fears the anti-aircraft guns opened up, battery after battery across the southern approaches to the station. When the guns around the camp perimeter started firing the roaring was on top of them.

No longer was there any of the old bravado of strolling towards the shelters. Men dashed to theirs and those who were slower off the mark found there was no room for them; the place was packed and they had to race for slit trenches elsewhere. Airwomen scampered to their shelter as if every alarm bell in their brains was ringing a high-pitched warning and they literally flung themselves inside. There they sat, mute and still.

The aircraft swept in almost wing tip to wing tip through and criss-crossing the barrage of fire that hammered up from the ground. Now the noise was fiendish, anti-aircraft guns pounding away without let-up, bombs exploding. There was a nightmarish quality about it all.

In the airwomen's shelter they could feel the earth trembling but they were remarkably calm. No panic, no hysteria, even when a bomb landed close to the entrance of the shelter and a hot pungent blast whooshed through and took their breath away. Another bomb fell closer still, the shelter rocked and then slowly the concrete walls caved in. Slabs, rubble and soil crumpled down upon the women packed inside like sardines. And then, somehow, as the earth stopped tumbling, the voice of a motherly flight sergeant was heard: 'My God! I think I've broken my back.' And then she added, 'And I've broken my false teeth too.' That brought the giggles. Now there was nothing to do but wait for the raid to end and to be dug out.

When the 'All Clear' sounded men raced to the airwomen's shelter. Pilots leapt from their cockpits to help. Slowly, carefully, the shelter was uncovered. One by one women were eased out. They were hardly recognizable, their faces as black as those of miners emerging after a long shift, and besmeared with blood, their clothes torn. By some miracle all were alive except one: Corporal Lena Button from Tasmania.

The airmen's shelter was a different story. It had been hit by one of the first bombs dropped in that raid, turning it into a gaping crater littered with mangled bodies and bits of bloody uniform.

Still Biggin Hill's ordeal was not over. Two more heroic airwomen would yet win a Military Medal.

True to form, German bombers arrived next day flying up-sun, at precisely six o'clock. In five minutes of concentrated bombing almost all of the buildings that still remained standing were flattened. Sergeant Helen Turner, a cheerful veteran of World War I, stayed at her switchboard in a small hut outside the operations room. A bomb landing outside her hut smashed most of the lines leading to her switchboard but, unmoved by this, Helen Turner managed to establish and maintain contact with 11 Group throughout the raid, until suddenly, when the bombing became even more intense, a huge rugby-playing sergeant took a flying tackle at Sergeant Turner and dragged her forcibly to the ground – just in time, for incredibly as it seemed later, a 500 lb bomb fell through the roof and bounced off the safe. It exploded in the next building where Corporal Elspeth Henderson was stubbornly sticking to her switchboard. The blast threw her on to the floor just as the group captain came into the room to see how everyone was faring. The same blast and flying debris knocked the pipe from his grasp. He grovelled about the floor, found it, stuffed it with tobacco and took a few tentative puffs before speaking to Corporal Henderson, praising her for her remarkable composure. 'There wasn't much I could do, was there Sir? After all, I joined the WAAF because I wanted to see a bit of life.'[14]

Section Officer Felicity Hanbury, a trim-figured athletic young woman, who was to receive the MBE for setting a magnificent example of courage and devotion to duty during the very heavy bombing attacks, made an interesting comment upon the heroism showed by her airwomen: 'When the bombing began and the Germans came down and machine-gunned the station, I think the girls were more frightened of showing they were frightened. They were determined not to let anyone down, no matter how terrified they were.'[15] The same might be said of her own actions. They were all sharing a fearful experience and a tremendous feeling of comradeship bound them together, giving them strength. Collectively they were all heroines in some way or other.

The same spirit fortified women on the anti-aircraft gun sites. Junior Commander Ruth Jewell recalled: 'It was a matter of pride for the girls of a mixed battery to do well in everything – on duty and off duty.'[16] And Major Jim Naylor, commanding 481 mixed AA Battery RA in one of the most active areas in the country at that time – Merseyside – said: 'There was no hardship the men faced that the girls weren't prepared to endure. Their pride and devotion to duty were really remarkable.'[17] That same devotion to duty was seen in eighteen-year-old Nora Caveney, a former factory worker who leapt at the opportunity of joining the front line anti-aircraft batteries when the chance was offered. She was following an enemy plane with her instruments during a raid and was on target when she was mortally wounded by a bomb splinter, but rather than lose her target she held on to it until the gun was fired. Then she collapsed, and died. Her place was taken immediately by another woman, who followed the track of the raiders, and the guns continued firing without a moment's delay.

Grace Catherine Golland, an ATS lance corporal in a heavy anti-aircraft regiment, set another inspiring example to all ranks. While she was on duty during a heavy raid, fifty incendiary bombs fell close around her, along with high-explosive bombs. Her citation for gallantry with the guns says: 'Despite the concussion from bombs and the heat and fumes engendered by the incendiaries, Lance Corporal Golland remained at her post and by her coolness and leadership enabled her team to maintain their duties, thereby allowing the site to fire in further engagements in a period of fifty-seven minutes.'[18]

All these women, from one 45-year-old farmer's wife to the eighteen-year-old gunner, were following their own intuition: 'that it seemed the right thing to do at the time'. It is clear in so many instances that bravery knows no gender (though women still cannot be awarded the Military or the Victoria Cross). Nothing would deter these women once they decided on a course of action.

When Pamela McGeorge, an eighteen-year-old WRN despatch rider, was delivering urgent messages and was caught in a heavy bombing raid on Devonport docks, she just carried on riding, weaving her motorbike round fire engines, over hoses and over rubble until the blast from one bomb blew her machine from under her. Flying debris damaged it so badly that she could no longer ride it. She could then legitimately have gone to a nearby naval shelter until the bombs had stopped falling but she still had her bag of despatches to deliver, so she abandoned her machine and delivered them on foot. The raid was still going on when she got back to her unit and immediately volunteered to go out again. Admiral of the Fleet, L.M. Forbes, recommended her for an award for valour in a citation, the last sentence of which reads: 'She displayed great gallantry, a high sense of duty and a complete disregard for her own safety.' She was awarded the British Empire Medal for doing, as she put it later, 'what I felt ought to be done in the circumstances'.

Putting one's life in jeopardy was a secondary consideration. It did not matter whether women were in military or civil formations. In that September of 1940 men and women of Civil Defence units rose to their Herculean tasks with unexampled courage and devotion. Many died at their posts of duty (the precise number will never be known), hundreds were injured; all worked hour upon hour through London's historic nights of bombardment without showing fear, without thought of self. Many brave acts by women Civil Defence workers and firewomen were never recorded, though the BBC recruited London firewoman, Audrey Russell, to make known their valour in regular broadcasts which turned out to be the prelude of a long and distinguished career. The government and the BBC realized how important it was for the public to know of the efforts their compatriots were making.

Young probationer nurses played an heroic part in rescue work when a hospital in south-east London was twice bombed in October 1940. High-explosive bombs cut through part of the kitchen quarters, devastating wards on both sides. Sister Hooker was putting a meal on a tray for a patient at the time and was killed outright. But those young nurses did not run for cover; they immediately began moving patients from damaged and blazing wards to other parts of the building. While they worked, bombers were still attacking. High explosive and incendiary bombs were falling all around. Shrapnel and debris cascaded through the open roof but they carried on doing what had to be done with a coolness and courage those young women never before knew they possessed.

So, as autumn came to Britain in 1940, the short dramatic chapter in her history came to an end and though bombs continued to fall on London and major cities in the provinces by night and the roll of the dead grew longer,[19] one thing gradually became clear: Hitler's 'Operation Sea Lion', the invasion of England, was off. Postponed for a few months, or perhaps for ever.

The German Reich Chancellor now had other plans: he was going to attack Russia. Britain had been too hard a nut to crack. In the words of the poster, Britain's courage, cheerfulness and resolution had contributed in no small way to the victory of 'The Few', that dwindling gallant company of RAF fighter pilots who were, in the summer of 1940, all that stood between Britain and defeat.

Supporting them were the 'Home Front heroines', taking risks regardless of their own safety. The courage they displayed typified what most British women wanted to believe was the true feeling of the nation. From the important aspect of the country's morale, there can be no doubt that their efforts gave it a tremendous fillip. Here were women doing something of which everyone could be proud.

Their heroism naturally raised the age-old question, the eternal question, of what it is that keeps us going in the face of horrific hazards?

A sense of 'fury' or 'outrage' at what was happening features largely in the recollections of many women who were commended for gallantry and there was the ever-present feeling of knowing it was the right thing to do in the circumstances.

There can be no doubt that those who were decorated for valour and the millions of anonymous 'unsung' heroines and heroes in the Services, like those who suffered the blitz and the German bombers, were men and women who defeated a deliberate attempt to break their morale. In doing so they discovered inner funds of resourcefulness and stamina that allowed them to concentrate on the immediate job to be done rather than on anxiety for their own safety. Thus, when chances of escape from hazards were offered, they chose the path of duty rather than that of self-preservation, often with tragic results.

Nowhere was this more evident that in a Coventry hospital in November 1940 and April 1941. Then it was that Hitler unleashed his bombers to raze every British city to the ground.

Now every man, woman and child was a potential victim of sudden death from the skies. In Coventry there were women who refused to be cowed – heroines in every sense of the word.

3

That Others Might Live

In the grey light of morning, nurses' bodies were found covering young children. They had died that others might live.

Rev. A.P. Wales, hospital chaplain

Harry Winter laid down his spoon with a sigh. 'Well, fellows,' he said, glancing round the table in the surgeons' dining room, 'I feel we're going to get it tonight.'[1]

For a moment he looked hungrily at the bowl of thick soup into which he had been about to dip his spoon for the first mouthful of a meal he had been looking forward to after a long session in the operating theatre, then he rose and walked purposefully over to the far wall where the control panel switches glowed. He flicked one of them. Immediately in wards and corridors throughout the Coventry and Warwickshire Hospital the yellow action stations light came on.

The warbling notes of the air-raid warning siren had sounded some minutes earlier but, as was the practice in that winter of 1940, hospital staff had carried on with the normal routine. There had been so many alarms without serious consequences – every time Birmingham was raided the Coventry siren went off too – that people paid little attention to the warning siren. In fact, when it went off during a Saturday afternoon Football League match between Coventry and Reading, the crowd forced the referee to let the game continue. As a result of this attitude to air raids, the hospital had developed its own air-raid warning routine of working normally after the siren sounded until the yellow light flashed on the colour signal code boards throughout the building, indicating 'danger imminent, go to action stations'.

Now anyone looking out of the hospital windows on that perfect moonlit night of 14 November 1940 could see why.

Floating down from throbbing German bombers were the first of their pathfinder chandelier flares. They were bursting above the city, making buildings stand out starkly like some brightly lit stage set. Everything was bathed in a pure white incandescent glow. And all around the hospital buildings incendiaries were whistling down.

Dr Harry Winter, aged twenty-eight, the resident surgical officer, was a tall, lightly built Canadian with alert black eyes and black hair receding prematurely from a high forehead. He had a black close-cropped moustache above a mouth that readily broke into a grin. He was not the sort of man usually given to gloomy prophecies. But on this particular night he had a premonition that they were all in for a really rough time. All the signs were there.

The German Luftwaffe, having failed to break the morale of Londoners after fifty-seven nights of consecutive aerial bombardment, were now evidently looking around for easier targets. Their raids were more widely dispersed throughout the island and clearly a major effort was now being made to cripple the industrial centres of Britain so as to break down the production of munitions and military equipment. Already the aero-engine works at Glasgow had endured several minor raids, as had the provincial industrial centres of Liverpool, Hull, Birmingham and Manchester. Now it seemed to Harry Winter, as it did to thousands of anxious citizens of Coventry, that this vital centre of the booming armaments industry could not escape the Luftwaffe's attention for much longer. It was surely a prime target.

Prime Minister Churchill however,[2] knew that it was not only a prime target but that it was *the* target for that night. Three days earlier, the Government Code and Cypher School at Bletchley had decoded German signals about a special raid code-named 'Moonlight Sonata' which was to begin on the night of the full moon. The target was *'Regenschirm'* (Umbrella). At first, Air Intelligence interpreted the code word to mean Birmingham, the parliamentary seat and home of former British Prime Minister Neville Chamberlain, who had nearly always been seen in photographs with his umbrella hooked over one arm. (Ironically and coincidentally, it was his funeral on 14 November, the day of the raid on Coventry.) Soon, however, another piece of information from a captured German pilot indicated that Coventry would be *the* target for the big raid.

Armed with this intelligence, gained mainly from the ability to read German secret codes following the capture of the Enigma coding machine, Churchill had the unenviable task of deciding whether to make special provision for Coventry's defence, thus showing the Germans that the British had cracked their secret codes, or to let the present defensive arrangements deal with the situation.

At 1500 hours on 14 November, RAF Fighter Command was warned that Coventry would be the target. No warning of the impending attack was sent to anyone in Coventry. Too much was at stake. The civil and administrative authorities there would just have to cope with their present resources.

So it was, that when Dr Harry Winter flicked on the 'yellow action stations' light, Matron Joyce Burton responded in her usual brisk manner. She had been appointed just two years earlier and though, like most matrons then, she was a strict disciplinarian, she was well respected and had established a system for dealing with air raids that her nurses of all grades operated most efficiently.

She was in matron's headquarters when her yellow light flashed. Immaculate as a Guards Brigade regimental sergeant major, she turned immediately towards the door but paused for a moment in front of a long wall mirror. She took a quick appraising glance at her reflection: not a strand of her brown, greying hair had dared escape from beneath her cap, her tightly fitted purple dress was wrinkle-free, her starched white collar precisely centred above the middle pleat of her dress. Then she walked swiftly towards the nearest of her wards – emergency or not, matrons do not run – to see for herself that everything was ship-shape and that the 'action stations' drills were being effectively carried out. Joyce Burton left nothing to chance.

Over on the medical ward, set apart from the main hospital complex, was Sister Emma Horne. She was a well-built, dark-haired Welsh woman who, when the yellow light went on, was seen to perform her characteristic response to any surprising situation. In one deft movement she raised her hand, pushed her glasses up the bridge of her nose and without pausing carried on to adjust the set of her triangular cap to the accompaniment of her strongest expletive: 'Well, drat my buttons!'

Neither of these two women appeared to be of that type seen in films who throw caution to the winds and completely disregard their own safety, to perform heroic deeds. Yet in the real-life drama of that long horrific night both of them would earn one of the highest civilian awards for valour: the George Medal.

Two miles away from the hospital at seven o'clock that evening, a seventeen-year-old probationary nurse, Edna Viner,[3] was just stepping off a bus to begin a rare treat – a whole evening away from the hospital. She had a late pass too that gave her until ten o'clock before having to be back in the nurses' home. Still in her first year of training, Edna worked cruelly long hours – from seven in the morning until nine at night – and apart from meal breaks she was on her feet all day, so that despite the sensible flat shoes they all had to wear, feet ached painfully and swelled over the shoe sides. That night however, Edna's feet were fine, a credit to the standard treatment of methylated spirits and talcum powder. For once she had got away from her ward on time but when she stood on the platform of her bus, ready to descend, she gazed about her in wonderment. The blacked-out city was strangely lit up in a silvery sheen. Then, once on the pavement, she looked up at the full moon rising in a cloudless sky. But it was not the moon alone which was responsible for the bright glare illuminating the houses, factories and three spires of the city. Dazzling white 'Christmas trees' were dropping beneath parachutes, shedding a bright white light, and powerful searchlight beams were criss-crossing the sky searching for the bombers. Already fire engines could be heard racing through the city streets, their bells clanging noisily. Added to the crescendo of noise there now came the sharp, clear bark of the Bofors anti-aircraft guns firing at the rate of 130 2lb rounds a minute.

Edna took in all these sights and sounds and came to a decision. She raced down the street towards her friend's house as fast as her young legs would carry her. She had just closed the door behind her when the first of the high-explosive bombs thudded down. Great buildings jumped into the air, disintegrating in blinding flashes of light. The cathedral was hit with high-explosive bombs and showers of incendiaries. Wardens and fire-watchers on roof-tops could see fierce orange and red flames spurting from windows and licking the walls of the slender tower, picking out the tiniest details.

Soon it seemed the whole of Coventry was resonating and shaking to the reports of bombs and guns.

Then, to the ears of Edna and her friends sheltering within the house, came the sound of someone hammering on the front door and a voice shouting urgently. They rushed to open the door just in time to hear the words of the air-raid warden flung over his shoulder as he dashed towards the next house. He was shouting: 'Get to the public shelter at once!'

Edna and her friends ran to the nearby reinforced public shelter through dense smoke and flakes of soot drifting thickly in the air like black snow, while all around fires roared and crackled. Silhouetted against the swirling smoke and blazing buildings were other families roused from their homes. Some carried hastily snatched bags, mothers hugged babies wrapped in overcoats or blankets, others dragged children by the hand.

The long night of terror and heroism had begun.

The main force of the German Kampf Gruppe 100 which had taken off from Vannes was now above the city. They had been directed exactly on to their target by the 'Knickerbein' transmitter on the French coast.[4]

Oberleutnant Manfred Deschner said:

> We simply steered along a sound beam, a radio signal. Dots and dashes in our earphones told us we were straying off course right or left and we got a continuous buzzing sound when we were spot on the exact bearing. I did two trips. After the first one I went back for another full load of high-explosive bombs but there was no need for the 'Knickerbein' on that second trip. We could see the crimson red glow in the sky soon after we crossed the English coast. It was far too awesome to be a pyrotechnic decoy to take us off course. And when we got over the target we could see everything so clearly, fires feeding off each other.[5]

Between Manfred Deschner's two trips, every bomber formation that Luftflotten 2 and 3 could muster was despatched against Coventry – 'a vital target, the centre of the enemy's armaments industry', according to the German operations order.

But when those pilots got to the conflagration and saw the white glare of the incendiaries bursting among the small houses of Coventry as well as the factories, the scene came as a shock. Many were appalled as they thought of what might be happening to the ordinary fathers and mothers, and children down below. There were many misgivings amongst the bomber crews. One of them reported on his return: 'The usual cheers that greeted a direct hit stuck in our throats. The crew just gazed down on the sea of flames in silence. Was this really a military target, we all asked ourselves?'

Dr Harry Winter gazed down too on those flames and could hardly believe his eyes.

> I went up three flights of stairs and out on to the flat roof of the main building. All around the hospital grounds glowed literally hundreds of incendiary bombs, like lights twinkling on a Christmas tree. Down below, in the light of other fires, which were already lighting up the sky over the city, I could see men of the hospital staff running from bomb to bomb, dousing them with buckets of sand.

Half a dozen small fires had started in the hospital building itself and the nurses' home was hit.

Sister Beti Price (now Mrs Howe) was in the bath when the first of the incendiaries fell.

> I was off duty that evening and planned to have an early bath and take some supper before the sirens sounded. But that was not to be. I was just relaxing in the hot water when the bombs started falling and the lights went out. I had to grope about in the glare coming in through the window to find some clothes to put on.[6]

Whilst the fire in the nurses' home was being put out, the rest of the nurses were evacuated to the main building. 'Again we were lucky,' recalled Dr Winter. 'No sooner had the last nurse left the building than a heavy high-explosive bomb crashed into it and exploded on the thick concrete top floor.'

By that time Sister Beti Price had reached her ophthalmic ward and was comforting her patients, attempting to keep them as unstressed as possible.

> There were many elderly men and women who had to be moved to a safer area. Normally eye patients had to be kept quite still after operations but we got them out of bed and hustled them in wheelchairs, on foot and on stretchers down to the ground floor of the main building. There they were made comfortable under the bed with a mattress over the top of them. The noise was horrendous and with the intense glare from

bursting incendiaries and the full moon, the newly painted part of the hospital, painted a brilliant white, stood out so prominently we felt hopelessly exposed.

Those nurses and doctors ferrying patients across the open space between the outside wards and the main building felt this exposure too, for high-explosive bombs as well as incendiaries were now dropping. But they were not put off. Here was a challenge they accepted as a matter of pride. A common idealism, a determination to maintain their long-established high standard, bound them together. Not one would ever have wanted the label of heroine attached to them but nevertheless, heroines they were.

Emma Horne, the strong Welsh sister of the medical ward, was particularly active in taking patients to safety. Ignoring the whizzing shrapnel from the anti-aircraft shells and the flying glass from the blasted windows, she crossed and recrossed those exposed areas. Dr Winter described the scene as doctors, nurses and hospital staff hurried to get patients tucked away in safer areas. 'Some crossed in wheelchairs, some on beds wheeled by nurses and some were hoisted on to shoulders and carried pick-a-back to the main hall. There was not a murmur from one of them,' he said, 'even though some of them must have been hurt with the jogging.'

As he reached the door of the main building with the last of the patients on his back he heard a bomb screaming down. It buried itself with a tremendous roar in the men's ward they had all just left and as he automatically turned round to see what had happened he saw the whole wall of that ward fall slowly outwards and crash on that same ground where they had all been scurrying moments earlier. 'Providence must have been watching over us,' he later recalled.

Sister Gladys Crichton has never forgotten those hectic moments nor the way the patients responded.

> I was at the other end of a stretcher carrying a man with leg injuries. Partly to console myself as well as the patient, I said, 'It won't be long, Dad.' He replied, 'Less of the Dad. I'm not even married.' I never did see his face, but he was so jolly lying on the stretcher looking up at Jerry passing over and saying, 'Hey, look at the fairy lights!'[7]

Patients that night could not find enough words of praise for the courage of those nurses and doctors. Mrs Evans of Green Lane, Coventry, was recovering from a major operation then and has never forgotten her ordeal and the way those nurses completely disregarded their own safety to look after their charges.

When the sirens sounded, nurses pulled our beds away from the windows to prevent us from being hit with flying glass and when the gun fire started they gave us bowls to put over our heads to protect us from flying debris. They had no protection whatever.

Suddenly there was a flash as an incendiary bomb crashed through the roof. It fell between three beds in a large bay window. The sister and a porter rushed over and pulled the beds away from where the fire had started. This they quickly put out but got burnt in the process.

By this time bombs were falling all around us. The lights went out and more incendiaries came. Then a bomb hurtled down on the side of the ward, covering the patients with glass and debris. The nurses got all the beds into a long corridor between the different wards. Then we were moved down to a new part of the building. Another woman was put into my bed, pillows were placed over our heads to protect us and the bed was put on to a theatre trolley. Our bumpy journey down to the new wing began, but half-way there we had to stop because of a fire in the corridor. Eventually we were all packed tightly together in the doctors' rest room, and for a brief moment or two everything seemed quiet. There was a loud explosion and the ceiling came down on us. Again the nurses were on the scene reassuring us and making us as comfortable as they could. Things went on like this until day break and at last came the peace we had prayed for. We heard a newly born baby cry.

The nurses, doctors, porters and staff were bricks and I must say I have never seen so much courage in all my life.

Reflecting on that night and the courage displayed, Sister Beti Price recalled her own strange reaction to it all.

It was frightening yet in a way I felt detached from it, like an onlooker at some frightful drama. I remember at one time in the middle of the raid in the early hours of the morning I was snatching a bite to eat and a cup of tea in the dining room and whilst I was sitting there I saw the curtains catch fire and swing lazily in the night breeze blowing in through the shattered windows. And the funny thing was I took it as nothing exceptionally frightening. Perhaps it was because I was young or just numbed. It was my twentieth birthday.

The raid went on. Hour after hour. Those who witnessed the raid from other parts of the city were just as numbed and mesmerized as Beti Price. The fires had an eerie fascination for them. Madge Faulkney, who worked on Spitfires in Birmingham and who was visiting friends in Coventry on that evening, recalled how they stood on tables to watch the spectacle. It grabbed and held their attention. 'I'd been through bombing before in Birmingham but it had not been anything like this. Look in any direction you wanted and all you could see were flames, flames, flames ...'[8]

Gradually, as the raid went on, the city's essential services broke down. Fire hydrants were buried under the debris of masonry and wooden beams. Water mains were shattered by bombs, and taps in houses produced only a dirty dribble. Such was the parlous state of water supplies that when future Mayor George Hodgkinson asked some firemen for a kettle of water from their hoses to make tea for the family, he was told that the water they were using came from the drains! Gas and electricity were the next to be knocked out and this caused tremendous problems in the hospital.

Sister Gladys Crichton was in Casualty when the electricity failed and all the lights went out.

I had to work by the light of hurricane lamps – ironically stamped 'Made in Germany' – and as we had no water either to boil we had to rely on Dettol to keep the needles, sutures and swabs sterile. The first of the casualties were firemen who had approached incendiary bombs just as they burst, hurtling fragments of hot metal which embedded themselves in their flesh. These men were brought in with faces soot black, streaked white where sweat or tears had run from smarting, inflamed eyes and their lips by contrast looked bright red where they had licked them. We just had to probe bits out from their faces and arms and stitch them up. Then many of them went back on duty again.

Some casualties were beyond any treatment we could administer and they were just given injections of pain-killing morphia. The dead were lying amongst the dying and the living. And those who were waiting to be treated could see what was happening. Man of the wounded on stretchers looked no different from the dead. In fact this caused a problem with one elderly woman. She had an open wound on her scalp that I could not cope with adequately in Casualty and so I took her along to the Outpatients Department where there was a little more room and better facilities. As we entered the doorway she took one look and shouted, 'I'm not going in there, they're all dead.' The only way I could convince her they were alive was to ask all of those lying on stretchers to raise their arms and show the lady she was amongst the living. Only then did she consent to being taken inside. I shaved her head, incised the black edges of the wound and stitched it together.

Joan Ottaway, who had begun her nursing training just one year earlier, was on duty on the resuscitation ward. Now she still remembers vividly the horrors of that night.

> In no time at all the ward was full. Shocked casualties were lying in great numbers all over the floor. Doctors and nurses worked at speed doing all they could for the injured but when morning came it was shocking to find how many had died as they lay there.
> I well remember one man who had been standing at a bus stop when a bomb fell nearby. A piece of debris had pierced his lung and his body gradually filled with air like a balloon. There was nothing that could be done to save him.[9]

For the medical staff of the hospital, hard at work, the time passed quickly but even to them it seemed the raid would never end. Bombs fell incessantly – history records that they were at intervals of less than a minute and went on for eleven hours.

There was a short period during the raid, probably about two o'clock in the morning, when the noise died down. This was probably the time that Mrs Evans noted in her own account. The reason for this quieter time was not because bombers had ceased to come over but that the 3.7 anti-aircraft guns had stopped firing. The citizens of Coventry were mystified. Were they to be left entirely to the mercy of the German Luftwaffe? Or was it that the crews had run out of ammunition? The truth was that the barrels were red hot and unable to fire any more.[10]

Surgeons and theatre sisters, using the emergency lighting system, worked all through the night in operating theatres which were bitterly cold as the frosty November air blew in through shattered windows. Dr Winter was in the middle of an operation when the emergency lighting failed. Quickly they rigged up a car headlamp to a battery and he finished the job. By this time though he was feeling pretty shaky and tired. He had had nothing to eat except a sip of soup since lunchtime the previous day and he had difficulty in keeping his hand steady.

> I wasn't exactly frightened but the sound of a bomb whistling down from five or six thousand feet above you isn't a comfortable one. Every few minutes the nurses and anaesthetist threw themselves under the operating table as the bombs roared down. Every time one whistled uncomfortably close I instinctively pulled the knife away and ducked sideways.

A soldier who was helping to bring casualties for emergency operations was crossing the courtyard for another patient when he received a direct hit from a bomb. The only trace of him ever having been in that hospital was the odd blood-stained piece of khaki uniform found later in the rubble, and a vague memory of his willing efforts. Nothing else. He had literally been blown to bits.

'The nurses were marvellous,' said Dr Winter later. 'With hurricane lamps and hand torches they moved among the patients, comforting them and giving them little sips of water.'[11]

Leading them, inspiring them, reassuring the younger ones all the time that night was Matron Joyce Burton. Never once did she sit down. Always on the move, always appearing where the situation was most critical, questioning in a quiet manner, listening and making positive suggestions. 'To me, as a very young probationer nurse then, she was as prominent and encouraging as a mobile lighthouse,' said one nurse.[12]

Here was leadership at its best. She was not quite so immaculate now. Her face, like those of so many of her nurses, would at any other time have been thought a ludicrous sight – smutty, smoke-stained, begrimed. Nevertheless it exuded confidence and a feeling that everything was under control. Her nurses had responded well to the challenge and were now eager to get back on duty, to the vocation that had called them as starry-eyed probationers, no matter what the hazards.

A new day dawned.

After eleven terrible hours the bombers turned and started to fly back east as daylight began to break through the smoky darkness, revealing the city in all its bomb-shattered mess. There was one last powerful crump of a high-explosive bomb followed by a sharp and clear bark of a 3.7 anti-aircraft gun hurling its final defiance. (They had already fired 6,700 rounds without bringing down one of the 449 bombers.) It was now six in the morning.

Faintly through the air-raid shelter doors the deep rumble of German aircraft engines, which had been the background to the night-long barrage, faded into nothing, leaving in its wake a quietness that was strange. Gradually then, other sounds intruded. Hoarse cries from the air-raid wardens could be heard as they walked through the drizzly rain: 'It's all over. All Clear!' With the electric power lines down the Civil Defence Headquarters were unable to sound the 'All Clear' on many sirens. Those that were working set up only a feeble whine. Other sounds joined the cries; the crunch and crackle of feet on broken glass as the dazed folk of Coventry tottered stiff-legged from their shelters rubbing their smoky eyes as they gazed in horror at scenes of desolation. They looked about hesitantly, wondering which way to go, still huddling in groups as if for comfort. After a few minutes though, the younger men and women began to stride purposefully, picking their way over debris and the dead, averting their eyes from limp bodies which were lying everywhere in unnaturally abandoned attitudes.

Probationer Nurse Edna Viner, whose late pass had expired at ten o'clock the previous evening, emerged haltingly from the foetid air of the shelter, blank-faced and dishevelled. Her one aim now was to get back to the hospital as quickly as possible.

It was not going to be easy. Fires still burned all over the city. Firemen, their eyes bloodshot and inflamed, stood by helplessly. There was no water. Even the canal, breached by the bombs, had been drained overnight.

As Edna walked apprehensively towards the hospital, wondering what she would find there, the route was tortuous. Many times she was diverted by police and wardens keeping her away from fires and unexploded bombs and it was difficult to recognize the once familiar streets.

Crowds of people were now returning home whilst others had but one thought in their minds: to get away. They trundled prams loaded with a few essentials over tangled masses of hosepipes. Some hardly knew where they were going, but going they were; getting away from a city they felt was doomed, into the quietness of the countryside. This was no panic-stricken exodus but a resolute withdrawal from a city that seemed to be writhing in its death agonies.

The casualties indeed had been terrible: at least 520 men, women and children had died and more than 1,200 were seriously wounded. Ambulance and stretcher men had been out in the streets all night but they still kept arriving at the Coventry and Warwickshire Hospital, bringing those in need of urgent medical attention.

When Edna Viner arrived at the hospital she was appalled at what she saw. Most of the windows had been blasted out, there were great gaps in some of the walls and not a door remained in its frame. The nurses' home was in ruins.

A roll call of nurses was about to be held to see how many had survived. Matron Joyce Burton somehow had managed to spruce herself up, determined to maintain the high standard of morale which had prevailed with patients and nurses throughout the night. Truly remarkable instances of fortitude were later recalled. Fifteen women on the top floor of the gynaecological ward who could not be moved, stayed in their beds throughout it all without complaint even though a high-explosive bomb smashed the staff headquarters next door and covered their faces and bed covers with glass from the windows and plaster from walls and ceilings. In another wing, patients with multiple fractures who also could not be moved lay immobilized on their backs, suspended in their frames, traction devices and splints, making wise-cracks as they watched German bombers cruising about the fire-lit sky through a large hole blasted in one of the walls.

'The morale was stupefying,' recalled Dr Winter. 'Throughout the packed hospital there was not one cry of fear, not a sign of panic. We did not have a case of hysteria all night long.'

A remarkable tribute indeed. But to whom?

The emergency had galvanized the whole hospital. Surgeons had operated non-stop with bombs thundering all around them. After a time no one bothered to duck. They just went on with the work, expecting every minute to have the building come down on top of them.

Sister Beti Price found that work was the only answer. 'There was nothing else we *could* do but get on with the job,' she recalled. 'All we could do was our best.'

Pride is a great motivator.

No wonder the patients responded with equal fortitude. The miracle of it all was that among all the patients and members of staff, not one was hit by the bombs. The only tragic casualty was the soldier who had voluntarily rushed into the hospital at the height of the bombing to see if he could help in any way. He had given his life.

No sooner had the roll call of nurses been completed than wardens rushed in with alarm written all over their faces to report that a delayed-action bomb had been found just outside the operating theatre. There could be others. Orders came for the whole hospital to be evacuated to other hospitals in the county of Warwickshire. Edna Viner and her colleagues went to Stratford-on-Avon.

Now, they felt, surely they could get on with their work in peace and quiet for the rest of the war. They had literally been through the fire, had been tested and had survived. Many indeed were amazed just how they had seemed to take it in their stride. They had been through a hellish experience and come through it uplifted, reassured about the capabilities of ordinary people coping with disaster. But they had now surely had enough for anyone's ration of terror.

Fate decreed otherwise. And the next time they would be mourning many lost colleagues.

When the aircrews of Luftflotten 2 and 3 got back to their bases in Vannes in their Heinkel 111H-3s bombers they were speedily debriefed and the news of their success was passed swiftly to Luftwaffe Commander Reichsmarschall Goering.[13] He was elated. Now surely Hitler would believe that the war could be won by strategic air attack alone and his Luftwaffe could do it if he were given the necessary support and power. Hitler was told of 'colossal devastations caused by bombs of heavy and superlatively heavy calibre', of 'monstrous conflagrations which were nourished by great stores of raw materials and were visible right up to the shores of the Channel, consummating the process of annihilation'.

Then Minister of Propaganda Dr Joseph Goebbels proclaimed: 'After this grand-scale attack by the Luftwaffe, the English coined a new verb: 'to coventrate'. By inventing this word which may be translated as 'to destroy utterly', they admitted the magnitude of the German victory.'

It was, of course, not the British press but the Germans who had given birth to the term 'coventrate'. The raid, however, was so serious that rather than have rumour-mongering making even more of it, the government lifted the restriction on the media naming a town bombed and full coverage was allowed. The day after the raid the *Daily Telegraph* reported that 'German bombers had made a concentrated night attack on the centre of the city and destroyed the Cathedral, except for its spire. Two hundred and fifty people were killed, eight hundred injured and hundreds left homeless.'[14]

Included in this article were the following words: 'A wonderful story of courage in a Coventry hospital during the raid was told later by Lord Leigh, President of the Coventry and Warwickshire Hospital, on whose behalf he made an appeal for financial help.'

The newspaper went on to relate how the big fires started in the hospital, spread rapidly to the various wards and how the nurses and staff miraculously moved patients from one building to another; it told how several of the male patients as well as nurses were engaged in putting out incendiary bombs. No mention was made of factories hit and the casualties were put at a much lower figure.

This did not convince the Germans however. They were so cock-sure that they had destroyed the city that they made the same big mistake as RAF Bomber Command was to make in 1942 when after their devastating raid on Cologne with a thousand bombers, they failed to go back on the second night when the city was still without adequate water for fire fighting and make a thorough job of the devastation. If Goering had sent his Luftwaffe to Coventry again the following night he could surely have administered the *coup de grâce*. Without water the city lay at the enemy's mercy, and the industrial plant which had escaped destruction would surely have been engulfed by the flames. But, deluded by their own pilots' reports and by the exaggeration of them as they were passed upwards from one headquarters to the next, all the German High Command did was gloat.

Within a surprisingly short time factories were at full production again. Nazi propaganda based on aerial photographs had said that 'Every single part of the Morris Engine Factory has been laid waste.' It certainly gave that impression to the interpreter of aerial photographs but the truth was that though roofs and walls had been destroyed the machinery was still comparatively untouched and within six weeks it was back to normal production.[15]

The Coventry and Warwickshire Hospital took a little longer to refurbish but at the beginning of April 1941 the nursing staff were brought back from the idyllic charm and peace of Stratford-on-Avon to resume duties in Coventry.

It was a time when the war news seemed good. Newspapers made much of the Royal Navy's success in the first great naval battle of the war which took place in the Ionian Sea off Matapan. Seven Italian warships including three 10,000 ton cruisers were sunk with losses of personnel reaching 4,000. British officers had entered Asmara, the capital of Eritrea, the RAF had bombed Brest where the German battle cruisers *Scharnhorst* and *Genisenau* were taking refuge, and in a raid on Emden the RAF had used for the first time a new type of high-explosive bomb of tremendous power. All very encouraging news.

The war, it seemed, had taken a turn for the better for Britain. So it was in an optimistic mood that those young nurses got back to the familiar surroundings of their old hospital. Little did they realize that within days they would have to face an aerial attack far more fearsome than anything experienced in November.

Sister Beti Price remembers that night so clearly. It was 8 April 1941, and she was on duty on Outpatients when the first bomb fell on the pharmacy next door. 'I can still recall that acrid smell of the cordite mixed with dust and debris that followed the explosion. I was pulled asunder, or so it seemed at the time and I felt numb but the thoughts going through my mind were: "Oh, how sad my parents will be when they hear I have been killed."'

In the operating theatre that night was Sister Gladys Crichton. Walls were shaking and glass was flying but the surgeon kept on with his tasks. She recalled:

At one time, we were all busy around the operating table treating a fireman for his burns. We had already given him the pentathol anaesthetic when we heard a bomb screeching down closer and closer. We cringed and flung ourselves to the floor as it burst so close to us. We could hardly believe our luck that we were still alive. Slowly we all stood up, dusted ourselves down a bit and prepared to carry on. But when we looked down at the table, the body of the fireman was no longer there. We stared at each other in amazement. Where was he? He had been blown right off the table and we found him on the floor still asleep under the anaesthetic. We picked him up, put him back on the table and continued dressing his burns. That man always kept in touch with us afterwards. In fact his daughter recently telephoned to say how he had never had any trouble at all with those burns after we had treated him!

A little later that night when the raid was at its worst, a bomb struck the X-ray department, killing a sister, a nurse and a patient.

'It became increasingly difficult to function at all after a while. Instruments were blown off the trolley on to the floor and it was impossible to keep things sterile,' said Sister Beti Price.

Staff were faced with the same problem in another operating theatre. Nurse Underwood and Mr Morton Anderson worked on that night until at last the dust from the crumbling building made it impossible for them to continue. All personnel left the operating theatre and Nurse Underwood began walking towards the basement hoping to reach the safety it offered. She would never arrive.

Survival was a matter of pure chance that night. Nurse Joyce Miles (now Testrail) was on duty in the men's ward.

> I had just laid out all the specimen glasses for the morning when the sirens went and so did the roof of the ward I was working on. I looked up to see the German pilots in their planes and I could imagine them laughing as they dropped their bombs on us. We had to work very quickly. The patients who could walk were taken to the basement. Those on drips or who were very ill, were moved to a corridor below. They were wonderful and called out, 'Under the bed, nurse!' as the bombers screamed around us.[16]

Nurse Ottoway and her friend Nurse Fortescue scrambled under a bed together with its former male occupant.

> The air was filled with shriek after shriek as the bombs fell thick and fast. Glass was splintering all around us. At two o'clock the raiders scored a direct hit on the very large medical cabinet in the centre of our long ward. There was a terrific explosion, followed immediately by screams and shouts for help. I felt the bed under which I was lying collapse on top of me, and a pain shot through my side. However, I was startled into action by the sudden appearance of a light beside me. I imagined, in the panic of the moment, that it was an incendiary bomb, but later realized it was the torch in my pocket which had been switched on by the blast. Nurse Fortescue was wounded in the foot but was able to get away unaided. Those of us who were able began to evacuate the last of those remaining in the ward. This was an experience in itself, as the walls of the corridor had been blown in at several places and through these gaps we could see the

orange glow of flames all over the city. We went backwards and forwards along this corridor until all the patients were taken care of, except, of course, those who had been killed, and then remained in the basement still tending the patients. The hours dragged by until at six o'clock we were thrilled to hear the 'All Clear' siren at last, and marvelled that we had come through such a dreadful night safely, though at the same time we were saddened by the remembrance of the many who had been killed or maimed, some of whom were our own colleagues.

Nurse Joyce Miles then was delighted to hear the voice of Mr Ballantyne, the senior gynaecologist, who had thoughtfully brought to the ward a primus stove and everything needed for cups of tea.

Some of the staff were already in the kitchen and called out to me, 'Miles, the tea is ready.' I was about to go and join them when a patient asked for a bedpan. I turned in my tracks and went for one for him. Suddenly there was a terrific explosion as a delayed-action bomb went off. The whole kitchen, with the staff in it, just disappeared. Patients at the end of the corridor were buried in rubble too. Nurses and patients in the basement were all killed. Two doctors on their way there were also killed. The first thing I saw was Sister Wilding [Tutor] scrabbling amongst the debris trying to uncover the injured. Dr Harry Winter, the resident surgical officer, called out to me, 'Get morphia, nurse!' We did our best with those whose limbs were showing through the rubble. I always say, a bedpan saved my life!

Just before that bomb exploded, Nurse Ottaway was on her way to the basement with her friend, Nurse Underwood, when she was stopped by a distraught father whose son, David, was in the children's ward. He was terribly anxious to know if his son was all right. Nurse Ottaway paused, told her friend to go on to the basement and then reassured the father right up to the door of the children's ward which had not been hit by high-explosive bombs.
They had only just parted company when the huge delayed-action bomb exploded. David's father was killed outright. Nurse Underwood was flung head over heels down the stone steps of the basement staircase and Nurse Ottaway was buried beneath a pile of bricks and masonry.

I felt myself being lifted into the air, and then I was conscious of a descent, at the end of which all was dark, and I was huddled in a semi-sitting position, with my hands in my pockets since it had been a very cold morning. My head was resting on a piece of debris, giving me a tiny space for breathing.

On finding myself in one piece I recalled reading in the newspaper accounts of buried people and decided the best thing for me to do was shout. This I began to do without delay. As nothing happened and I became more breathless, I stayed quiet for a while, but as time went on my situation began to get desperate. The weight of the debris on me was very considerable, and it made it difficult for me to expand my chest for inhaling. I could not move any part of me, but worst of all, the little oxygen I had in the gap in front of my face was getting used up. Breathing began to be laboured. I called again, once or twice, but it was obvious that no one could hear me, so I began to feel my end was near.

I was perfectly peaceful as I thought about death. I had no fear. I had to put my trust in Christ for salvation, and felt confident that very soon I would be in the presence of God. My breath was coming hard in gasps by this time, and I was getting very weak. I had no idea what was going on outside my dark grave, and wondered if my friend would be looking for me, not knowing that at that time she lay prostrate with a heavy door on top of her and with her skull fractured.

One and a half hours after the bomb exploded, when my end was as near as seemed possible, I was suddenly aware of voices and activity not too far away. I felt the weight of the debris increase on me – men were walking over me not knowing I was there. I made a supreme effort to shout once more. I heard someone say, 'It's all right, old man, we will soon have you out', and I smiled to myself, thinking of the surprise they would get when they found that I was a nurse. I didn't realize they were talking to an old man who was in a bed that rested across my numbed knees. As they freed him and were about to carry him away, I shouted again, and just as the rescuers were leaving they heard my shouts. I heard one of them say, 'There's someone else down there!' I knew then I would be saved.

Strangely enough, my first reaction was one of disappointment at being, as it were, snatched from the gates of heaven!

I was extricated from the debris, put on a stretcher and taken to the casualty department, where I was surrounded by others on stretchers. We were given a cup of tea and an anti-tetanus injection and finally taken to the comparative safety of a hospital in Leamington Spa. On the following day I had the thrill of being visited by the Duchess of Gloucester.

In a bed nearby, lay Joan Ottaway's friend, Nurse Underwood, with a fractured skull.

Joan Ottaway was not the only one buried alive that morning. So too were nurses and patients who had been taken to the basement for safety. Only a few were rescued alive. One of that rescue team, Mr Joseph Ryan, remembers the awful job they had in trying to get to those trapped and mangled bodies, through the underground corridor which had collapsed.

> When we were inside that dark tunnel it seemed endless. Stooping to save our heads from a mass of pipes, we forged on for what seemed an eternity. We got the impression there was not a living soul there but ourselves but then we heard groans and yes, there was life there, and sad to relate, death too. Quickly the victims were passed from hand to hand through the pipes to safety. I remember how a little child would not release its hold of a rescuer until the soothing voice of a nurse coming out of the darkness bade her come, and how another poor soul kept calling for his nurse not knowing that the gallant woman shielding him with her body was rapidly dying. Never will I forget those men and women, caring not for personal safety and proving the truth of the saying: 'The rent of life is service.'

Sister Joyce Evans was trapped beneath a mound of concrete at the end of a narrow tunnel made by the rescue workers. They could see her feet sticking out but not one of the rescue team could stretch far enough to reach her. 'Send for long-reach Ryan,' shouted the team leader. Ryan, a Corporation bus driver and rescue-team man, stood six-foot four in his stockinged feet and had arms to match his height. He struggled forward through the narrow gap. He pulled her so far out, turned her round and then dragged her out head first. 'I had to almost scalp her, and once I had got her free, she just clung to me, grateful to be alive,' he recalled.[17]

Early on that April morning after the raid, when the mist mingled with the acrid smoke and singed dust, people began to gather and gawp at the ghastly scene of desolation at the hospital; at the heaps of bricks and timber, fallen walls, charred rafters, shattered windows and firemen's hoses snaking over the glass-filled approach roads which were now roped off.

Beyond those ropes, however, traffic was moving, the city was coming alive again, the routine of life was pulsating once more. Order was being restored.

Matron Burton had her own way of re-establishing routine.

She held a roll call in the laboratory, to find out again how many other nurses had survived. It was a sad time that Sister Price remembers still: 'The girl who had relieved me on night duty was lying dying. I was angry, blazing angry that she should be so young and dying. I spoke to the surgeon, wanting something to be done. He just looked at me for a moment, without speaking, and then said simply that nothing could be done. She was indeed, just dying.'

There was nothing to be done either with the hospital then. It was unusable; the building was wrecked, its staff depleted. It was left to Matron Burton to give instructions to the nurses. They were brief. 'If you have anywhere to go, leave your name and address and go. Just go.'

And so they went. One by one, carrying their few possessions in battered suitcases, they trudged off alone on their separate ways as the last splinters of glass fell tinkling from shattered window panes and fragments of plaster fluttered down in the gentle spring breeze.

Those who looked back at the shell of the hospital in which they had served, marvelled that they had stuck it out through the dreadful night. For these were just ordinary people who never dreamed of striking attitudes and being brave. Yet they had become extraordinary, full of that spirit that rises in people when the testing time comes – courage. The stuff of heroes and heroines.

They could not all be given medals and so George Medals were awarded to their representatives – Matron Joyce Burton, Sister Emma Horne, and the Hospital House Governor. It was recognition of everyone's extraordinary and gallant devotion to duty.

There would be other challenges for these men and women to meet, for the war's end was still a long way off and the news now was far from good. It was a grim-faced Deputy Prime Minister, Clement Attlee, who rose to give it to the House of Commons that first week of April 1942. He told of mounting merchant shipping losses, of 39,856 civilians killed by bombing, of 37,607 fighting forces dead and finally of yet another disaster looming as a defeated British and Commonwealth Army fought to withdraw its forces from a disastrous campaign in Greece.

It would be there, in Greece and Crete, that yet another young woman, also a nurse, would display remarkable courage which would earn accolades from two countries for gallantry in the field.

4

Nurse Under Siege

It is not easy to visualize valour such as this, she was
as tough as any man and as tireless as the fittest of
them. Utterly fearless.

Colonel Hamilton Fiarley, RAMC,
on English nurse, Joanna Stavridi

Six o'clock on the morning of 20 May 1941. Behind the razor
back of the eastern ridge of hills, a bright orange sun blazed on
to the faded tents of the British 97th General Hospital, set
almost on the sea shore between Crete's capital and major port,
Canea, and the Maleme airfield. The sky was flecked blue, the
air clear and cool with a soft breeze which rattled thick clumps
of reeds and gathered dust into swirling eddies by the tent
doorways. There was an uncanny stillness about the camp in
which occasional noises came harsh and with an echoing
quality: the clatter of cookhouse baking trays, a raucous voice
raised, and a sudden cry from a patient disturbed in his sleep.

It was one of those deceptively pleasant days when nature
conspires to lull the unwary into a sense of peacefulness with
the world. But to the tall, sun-bronzed nursing sister standing
at the end of the largest marquee, the morning scene could
have given no peace of mind. Far from it. She had seen too
much of death and destruction lately.

The tall nurse's name was Joanna Stavridi. Daughter of a
London banker, she was a strong-looking girl with magnificent
black hair tucked under her crisp, white nurse's cap. She had
left London a little over a year ago and it was hard for her to
believe that she was now acting matron of the tented British
97th General Hospital – the only woman left there and with 700
beds in her charge.

As she braced herself for the walk round the wards that
morning and for the horror she feared must soon begin, her

feelings surely comprised a mixture of tense anxiety and excitement. This unfamiliar quiet would not last for long. Whilst walking between the rows of beds it would have been surprising if her mind had not wandered back over the chain of events which had brought her to this strange situation. Events which, in the next few days, would make her a heroine.

It had all begun maybe two years earlier, or even before that. One thing is certain, however: in those years of crises and suspense just before the Second World War began, when Joanna was at home in London, she was utterly bored as 'a society butterfly'.[1]

Although she was thirty years old she had not yet found her path in life. 'She was a highly intelligent, gifted girl who, with her diplomatic background and great popularity, one expected to become the wife of an ambassador,' said her English cousin and friend, Mrs Margaret Stavridi.

Of course she had taken a job; she was doing well lecturing in fabric design at art college, but already she felt there must be more satisfying tasks, especially now war was approaching, for her to tackle. And the social side of her financially privileged life no longer had much appeal; she had been presented at court, attended debutante parties until two or three in the morning, but it had all seemed empty, purposeless. Now she was ready to play a more worthwhile role. But what?

She was, more than any of her contemporaries, aware of the serious crisis facing the country. Earlier in the thirties, cinema news reels showing German bombers strafing Spanish cities and the Japanese bombing Shanghai had made a vivid impression on her and she could see that Britain herself was no longer inviolate simply because no invader had entered London's gates since William of Normandy. She believed the time would be not too distant when her beloved Britain, and its capital, would be in peril from a new threat by sea and even, for the first time, from the air. But what part could she play in what was to come?

She had no particular technical skills or professional qualifications. If she volunteered for the women's services now being formed, would the tradition which rigidly excluded women from male spheres confine her to what she thought would be the drab routine of catering, clerking, or general duties? The idea did not appeal to her at all. She wanted to escape from the conventions of her femininity. Indeed, she

Signposts were removed to
make travel for invaders more
difficult

Invasion imminent!
Roadblocks, manned by the
Home Guard, were set up to
search cars which might have
been commandeered by
parachutists to sabotage
installations

Corporal J.D.M. Pearson, WAAF, EGM.
From a painting by Dame Laura Knight

YOUR COURAGE
YOUR CHEERFULNESS
YOUR RESOLUTION
WILL BRING
US VICTORY

A wing of the notorious Fresnes prison in Paris. It was one of the biggest criminal prisons in Europe. When Paris fell to the Germans in 1940 it was taken over by the SS and their sisters, the women in grey — *les sourirs* (the mice). Here Diana Rowden was first imprisoned

The concentration camp ovens in which Diana was burnt

Women concentration camp guards face No. 1 War Crimes Court, Hamburg, 10 December 1946. Front row: Dorothea Binz (executed), Margaret Mewes (ten years prison), Greta Bosel (executed), Eugene von Skene (ten years prison). Back row: Elizabeth Marschall (executed), Vera Salvequart (executed)

Diana Rowden, Croix de Guerre

1939   **1945**

IN HONOURED MEMORY OF THOSE MEMBERS OF THE
WOMEN'S TRANSPORT SERVICE (F·A·N·Y.)
WHO GAVE THEIR LIVES FOR THEIR KING AND COUNTRY.

M.W.ANDERSON	M.DAMERMENT C de G	M.M.M°KENZIE MILLIGAN	E.G.SADLER
Y.E.M.BEEKMAN C de G	B.M.DICKIE	D.MORGAN	H.I.P.SALMON
D.BLOCH	B.E.EBDEN	R.E.NELSON	J.SHEPLEY
E.M.BOILEAU	M.HEATH-JONES	M.C.PEAKE	L.M.STALKER
A.BORREL	J.HILDICK-SMITH	E.S.PLEWMAN C de G.	E.P.STANGER
M.S.BUTLER	N.INYAT-KHANG.C	B.E.RAMSAY	N.C.STAPYLTON
M.BYCK	C.LEFORT	F.L.RAWLINS	B.SWINBURNE-HANHAM
C.E.CLERK-RATTRAY	V.E.LEIGH	L.V.ROLFE C de G.	V.R.E.SZABO G.C.
C.D.CROOKE	C.M.LOPRESTI	D.H.ROWDEN C de G	M.J.THOMPSON
K.CROSS	D.M.MANNING	Y.RUDELLAT	P.C.WOOLLAN
	NÉE PORTMAN		C.M.BRADFORD (IN JAPAN) 7.5.1947

W.T.S. (EAST AFRICA)

B.M.AUSTIN	B.DUNBAR THOMSON.	B.KENTISH	M.SYKES
A.CALLISHER	W.GREY	F.F.MOOJEN	P.H.LE POER TRENCH
	H.C.CAMERER	S.HOOK	R.SOUTHEY

THEIR NAME LIVETH FOR EVERMORE.

On the wall of St Paul's Church, Knightsbridge, is the memorial
tablet to those who died for their country. Diana's name is in
column three

King George VI and Queen Elizabeth (now the Queen Mother) present Eveline Cardwell with her award for gallantry. *Above*: Eveline's medal, cherished now by her daughter

Notices warning people about the possibility of invasion by German forces were posted up in many coastal towns in 1940. Note how detailed are the instructions to various categories of personnel

Where the parachutist landed in Eveline's garden

DANGER of INVASION

Last year all who could be spared from this town were asked to leave, not only for their own safety, but so as to ease the work of the Armed Forces in repelling an invasion.

The danger of invasion has increased and the Government requests all who can be spared, and have somewhere to go, to leave without delay.

This applies particularly to :—

SCHOOL CHILDREN
MOTHERS WITH YOUNG CHILDREN
AGED AND INFIRM PERSONS
PERSONS LIVING ON PENSIONS
PERSONS WITHOUT OCCUPATION
OR IN RETIREMENT

If you are one of these, you should arrange to go to some other part of the country. You should not go to the coastal area of East Anglia, Kent or Sussex.

School children can be registered to join school parties in the reception areas, and billets will be found for them.

If you are in need of help you can have your railway fare paid and a billeting allowance paid to any relative or friend with whom you stay.

If you are going, go quickly.

Take your
NATIONAL REGISTRATION IDENTITY CARD
RATION BOOK
GAS MASK

ALSO any bank book, pension payment order book, insurance cards, unemployment book, military registration documents, passport, insurance policies, securities and any ready money.

If your house will be left unoccupied, turn off gas, electricity and water supplies and make provision for animals and birds. Lock your house securely. Blinds should be left up, and if there is a telephone line, ask the telephone exchange to disconnect it.

Apply at the Local Council Offices for further information.

Private Car and Motor Cycle owners who have not licensed their vehicles and have no petrol coupons may be allowed to use their cars unlicensed for one journey only and may apply to the Police for petrol coupons to enable them to secure sufficient petrol to journey to their destination.

ESSENTIAL WORKERS MUST STAY
particularly the following classes :—

Members of the Home Guard
Observer Corps
Coastguards, Coast Watchers and Lifeboat Crews
Police and Special Constabulary
Fire Brigade and Auxiliary Fire Service
A.R.P. and Casualty Services
Members of Local Authorities and their officials and employees
Workers on the land
Persons engaged on war work, and other essential services
Persons employed by contractors on defence work
Employees of water, sewerage, gas & electricity undertakings
Persons engaged in the supply and distribution of food
Workers on export trades
Doctors, Nurses and Chemists
Ministers of Religion
Government Employees
Employees of banks
Employees of transport undertakings,
namely railways, docks, canals, ferries,
and road transport (both passenger and goods).

When invasion is upon us it may be necessary to evacuate the remaining population of this and certain other towns. Evacuation would then be compulsory at short notice, in crowded trains, with scanty luggage, to destinations chosen by the Government. If you are not among the essential workers mentioned above, it is better to go now while the going is good.

AUCKLAND GEDDES,
REGIONAL COMMISSIONER FOR CIVIL DEFENCE,
TUNBRIDGE WELLS.
MARCH, 1941.

Gladys Spencer Crichton, *(right)* Edna Viner and *(centre)* Joan Ottaway, probationer nurses at the time of the Coventry blitz

Nurses the next morning, with a makeshift blackboard notice, carry on work in the ruins of the hospital

ACCIDENT CASES THIS WAY PLEASE

Dunley Manor,
Whitchurch,
Hants.

2nd May, 1941.

Dear Nurse Price,

Lady Herbert and I have been filled
with admiration for the courage and self-
sacrifice displayed by yourself and your
colleagues during the recent heavy raid
on the Hospital. The work that you did
in this great emergency for the patients
under yourcare can never be forgotten.

As a small token of my appreciation
and respect, I shall be grateful if you
will kindly accept the enclosed.

I hope that your health has not
suffered as a result of that terrible
experience.

With all good wishes,

Yours sincerely,

Alfred Herbert

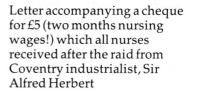

Letter accompanying a cheque for £5 (two months nursing wages!) which all nurses received after the raid from Coventry industrialist, Sir Alfred Herbert

Dr Harry Winter (holding X-ray negative) and staff at Coventry Hospital

Matron Miss J.E. Burton accompanying the King and Queen on their visit to Coventry and Warwickshire Hospital. Many of the nurses acting as guard of honour then were present fifty years later when the Queen Mother made a return visit to Coventry Cathedral

The hospital after the blitz,
April 1941

On the morning after the raid, Nurse Edna Viner and others
had to pick their way through the remains of what had once
been a busy thoroughfare to report for duty

bridled at the restrictions society placed on women, for Joanna was a rare creature in those days. She was an ardent feminist. Not for her was the notion that a woman's place was in the home, cooking and looking after children, which seemed to be the accepted philosophy in 1939. For all the efforts of Mrs Pankhurst and her suffragette campaign, what had really been achieved? Votes for women and, until 1940, rarely more than a dozen women Members of Parliament. After years of campaigning what had actually been done to break down the barriers to equality between the sexes? Precious little. Women were still second-class citizens, financially and socially.

In 1939 many professions were still trying to keep women out; in factories their wages were not on a level with men's for the old-fashioned reason that a man might have to keep a wife and children.

Women were handicapped on all sides by traditions of the social code which simply did not acknowledge women's claim for equality of reward and opportunity. Despite having proved themselves by their work in front line ambulance services under fire, in hospitals and in factories in the First World War they were still, twenty years later, not allowed to compete with men on equal terms. No wonder women like Joanna felt they had had more than their fill of being worshipped for their weakness, patronized for their timidity and adored for their dependence upon man's strength and chivalry. All that, Joanna found, was boring and enormously irritating.

Joanna's irritation was to grow with her experience of war, as will be seen, and she expressed her feelings forcibly to her father in a letter from the battle front:

> If this war has done nothing else it's made me a much more ardent feminist than ever before. We women have had to sit by and watch all we cared for and loved smashed to smithereens and haven't been allowed a say in the matter. I trust and hope that we shall rise up in a battalion when it's over and insist on having an equal say in the future arrangements of the world, so that we may stop men making fools of themselves and wrecking our homes and killing our husbands and children.

But all that was in the future.

In September 1939 when Britain declared war on Germany, Joanna felt the need to be personally involved in her country's battle against the evil of National Socialism for although her family hailed from Greece, three generations back, Joanna above all loved England and she was furious that Britain had done so little to prepare itself for the war which everyone in the late 1930s could see coming. She feared for Britain's future. 'I know,' she wrote, 'that England and the English matter to me more than anything else in the world.'

In such a mood she found those first few months of inactivity after war was declared irritatingly boring; even the British public was beginning to call that period the 'Bore War' or 'Phoney War'. She wanted to be doing something for the war effort. She had volunteered her services to a Chelsea First Aid Post but there was nothing for her to do there. Everyone had expected that London would be bombed violently straightaway and that there would be enormous casualties. Consequently many of the hospitals there were cleared of bed cases who were evacuated to hospitals sixty miles away from the city. The vacated beds were kept in readiness for the estimated 30,000 casualties a day. Now they stood empty.

At first, all over London there was an uneasy feeling that life had stopped; that people were just waiting for something to happen. Thousands of Londoners had taken their families to safe areas in the country and no one who could help it came up to London. But, within a short time, in the absence of raids people began to drift back again; theatres and cinemas which had closed on the outbreak of war opened again. Surprisingly, everything seemed quiet. It was a complete anticlimax.

From that artificial and boring life, and the oppressive confines of an over-protective family, Joanna longed to escape and make her own way. Her father doted on her – though he did not believe education was as important for a daughter as for a son.[2] Her mother was domineering and possessive to the extent of demanding to know who had written any letter that came for Joanna and had even forbidden her to attend 'life' drawing classes when she was an art student.[3]

Her first steps towards the battle front began early in 1940 when she enrolled for training as a nurse but before she could complete her course in London, Fate stepped in with news from Greece. Her sister Dolly, married to a Greek minister living in Athens, fell ill and lost her little twin boys. Now here was the opportunity for Joanna to have practical experience in nursing and also for her to escape from the ties of the family. It was an opportunity to take off on an exciting journey.

Unwittingly, she travelled to war in style. She boarded the

Orient Express in London and arrived in Athens in good time to help her sister through her illness. Afterwards, she lingered on, enjoying the Greek summer and early autumn, whilst Dolly convalesced. During this time she took her nursing training with the Greek Red Cross and passed all her examinations with distinction.

She was just beginning to wonder when she should go back to Britain and indeed had just written to her father to ask what he thought when Fate yet again took a hand in her affairs. This time it was in the form of an unexpected outrage committed by the Italian dictator, Mussolini. Tempted by the prospect of a quick and easy conquest of Greece, he ordered the Italian army in Albania to cross the Greek frontier without any warning whatsoever, before dawn on 21 October 1940.

Immediately, King George of the Hellenes, now back on the throne after twelve years living in the comfort of Brown's Hotel, London, invoked the guarantee given by Britain to Greece in April 1939. King George VI of Britain himself replied: 'We will fight a common foe and will share a common victory.'[4]

The most immediate contribution to that promised help came from Joanna Stavridi herself. Away from home she was now her own woman, self-reliant and emphatic. She volunteered for service at the front line with the Greek Red Cross, on the Albanian–Greek frontier where the Greek troops were putting up a magnificent defence. The Italian army, which had been promised an easy victory by Mussolini, was soon to learn that against them was a brave and resolute enemy who could take full advantage of the difficult and rugged country. Ill-equipped though they were, the sturdy Greek infantry held the Italian invaders (who were also poorly equipped for the task) in fighting that at times was fierce and hand to hand. Joanna served on the hospital trains which ran as close to the front as possible, evacuating the wounded from front-line casualty clearing stations which themselves were frequently under shell fire. Sometimes too she served in the operating theatre of the advanced field hospitals and there she discovered the satisfaction that comes to the truly dedicated nurse. While she was employed in the operating theatre at Arta she was frequently at risk of being encircled by desperate flanking attacks mounted by the crack Italian mountain troops brought in for the task. But at last the invaders were brought to a halt at Janina and the Italian attack was turned into a rout.

For a few weeks Greece celebrated its victory, and feted its gallant army which had humiliated the Italians. Meanwhile, Joanna took further training with the military side of the Greek Red Cross.

Then the Third Reich took a hand.

In April 1941 fifteen German divisions attacked the Greek defences in Macedonia. Britain hurriedly despatched a token force of 53,000 troops but neither they nor the Greeks could hold the German onslaught. Within a short time the British and Commonwealth divisions were hustled back to their ships in the south. Another Dunkirk. On 27 April German tanks rattled into Athens and the swastika was hoisted over the Acropolis. Joanna just beat them to Athens where her brother, Valieri, who worked for the British Information Service in London, had somehow pulled strings to arrange for her to be evacuated with the Embassy staff in a yacht leaving Piraeus.

It looked as if Joanna's military adventures were now at an end. Far from it; they were only just beginning. She sailed in the yacht on 23 April along with Colonel Neil Hamilton-Fairley of the Royal Army Medical Corps and began an ordeal of running the gauntlet of German dive bombers. The colonel later reported, in cold objective military language, what happened.

> We left at night in a small boat and after being bombed throughout the first part of the journey, reached the small island of Kimolos. Next morning, we landed there to await the evening when we were to continue our journey to Crete. At about six in the evening we were having tea under a tree when a plane flew over very low dropping bombs and machine-gunning us. Our ship received a direct hit and went up in flames with all our belongings. Two of the crew of twelve were killed and the rest badly burned.[5]

For four days they waited for another boat to arrive to take them to Crete. During all this time Joanna tended the six badly wounded men. At last the boat came and took them to the Crete port of Canea. Their troubles were then only just beginning.

The Luftwaffe's fighter bombers gave them no rest whatsoever for it was at this time that freighters began to arrive from Greece bringing troops evacuated from the beaches. Amongst them was one ship which arrived in Suda Bay crowded with wounded and eighty nurses from British and Australian hospitals.

The nurses were from No. 1 General Hospital which had been close to the front line in Greece catering for 1,000 patients[6] and during the long retreat to the beaches had withstood gruelling and almost continuous attacks from the German Air Force. After a perilous embarkation they were relieved to land on Crete but were eager to return to active service as soon as they could. Typically, they said, 'Active service gets right into the blood.'[7]

Wounded then began to arrive in all kinds of craft: naval ships, caiques, sailing dinghies, yachts. After weeks under the stress of battle, men who had been close to death found temporary haven and gathered to give thanks for their deliverance in a service of thanksgiving on the rocky ground outside the hospital. A large rock draped with the Union Jack served as an altar supporting a simple wooden cross flanked by two jam jars filled with wild flowers. Together the voices of nurses and wounded men joined in singing the hymn, 'Oh God our help in ages past'. An apt choice.

Soon that help was going to be needed again.

On the second night after their arrival, nurses were awakened by a sergeant shouting orders for all nurses and the walking wounded to be ready to leave by daybreak. Bedding was rolled, kits packed, columns formed, further orders filtered through the commotion and slowly the evacuation went ahead. According to plan, at nine o'clock the following morning, the ancient steamship *Iona* sailed packed with wounded and all the nurses except one.

Joanna Stavridi had chosen to stay behind.

The moment of truth for her had arrived. She had, on that 13 May, been about to leave on the ship for Cairo when the officer commanding the 97th General Hospital heard that there was a Red Cross nurse in Colonel Hamilton-Fairley's party. He was in desperate need of a nurse to look after the seriously wounded personnel. It was almost as if Fate had determined that Joanna Stavridi should be a heroine.

Colonel Hamilton-Fairley described how it all happened.

The authorities told us that we could not stay any longer on the island. We made arrangements to leave for Cairo on 14 May. Joanna was to come with us. Then the commanding officer of 97th General Hospital hurried across to see us. He had a proposition to make. Would Joanna stay as matron in charge of the seriously wounded? She was to be the only woman there in the 700-bed hospital. When we parted from her on the 13th it was horrible, but there was little we could do to dissuade her. She was desperately keen on her work and so completely fearless.[8]

'Keen'? 'Fearless'? The basic truth of the notions of courage and fear only becomes clear in the stress of battle. Then individuals have to establish a working compromise between a sense of duty and the instinct for self-preservation. Those who cannot achieve this and let the instinct for self-preservation dominate, break down. True courage can be seen in those who have already experienced the stress of being shelled, bombed and shot at and yet carry on quietly doing their duty. Joanna was typical of them.

A little to the south of the 97th General Hospital, on the morning of 20 May 1941, Brigadier Kippenberger, of the Second New Zealand Division, was shaving and wondering at the same time just how much longer his war-weary infantrymen would have before they were called upon to face yet another battle.[9] They had been brought over to Greece from the Western Desert, where they had already suffered heavy losses, and in three punishing weeks in Greece, had endured one defeat after another in which much of their equipment had been lost. Now the remnants of New Zealand and Australian divisions had been reorganized into makeshift infantry units. They were formed out of gunners who had lost their guns, sappers who had lost their tools, and RASC drivers who had lost their cars. Such was the lack of equipment that men had to use their steel helmets to scoop out slit trenches.

Worse still, they were all hungry. Rations were not coming through.

Brigadier Kippenberger was a worried man that breakfast time. He was eating a thin gruel of oatmeal and water when suddenly his liaison officer, seated opposite him in the makeshift mess, broke the breakfast silence rule and swore loudly. Kippenberger, unused to officers talking at breakfast time, even on active service, looked up, his spoon poised midway between plate and mouth. He stared aghast, as if unable to believe his eyes. He was looking at something far more disturbing than the errant officer. 'Almost over our heads were four gliders, the first we had ever seen, in their silence inexpressibly menacing,' he recalled.[10]

Kippenberger's liaison officer was not the only one to be swearing that morning. Twenty miles to the east, Captain Roy Farran, with a squadron of battered, patched-up tanks of the 3rd Hussars, had been looking forward to a pleasant day. They had just arrived from Egypt and were encamped in the comparatively cool shade of olive trees overlooking Suda Bay harbour.

To Farran and his men, all of whom had spent long months in the monotonous barren wastes of the Western Desert, Crete seemed like paradise. Indeed it was. Rising out of the eastern Mediterranean, that mountainous island – 180 miles from east to west – had so many contrasting landscapes to offer. And when Farran and his men arrived Crete was in its glorious though short period of greenness. The days were mild with the coming of spring and wild flowers were patching the slopes of the White Mountains and Mount Ida with colour. The tank troopers wondered what they had done to deserve the break in a land where there were not only trees and sunny beaches but also mountains still snow-capped in May. The villages were untouched by modern life and foraging troopers had already found means of supplementing their meagre army rations. 'There were sheep to be bought, handsome smiling peasants and, above all, the cool shade of trees to lie under,' recalled Farran.[11]

The hardy Cretans took this friendly invasion in their stride, going on with the daily work of cultivating their vines, ploughing the red soil, herding their sheep and goats.

Villagers sold cool coarse local wine to the troops and as Farran recalled, 'There were pretty girls in light summer frocks who, true to the traditional hospitality of Cretan people, were not at all averse to responding cheerfully to soldiers who chatted them up. Strangers were, as they always had been, welcome guests.'

Captain Roy Farran and officers of the 3rd Hussars had set up their mess under a shady olive tree and they were sitting at a deal table eating breakfast in a civilized manner when suddenly there was a roar of aircraft and the sky was filled with dive bombers and fighters. They swooped down out of the sun like angry hornets. The whine of the bullets, rattle of machine guns and the scream of falling bombs shattered the morning quiet. Never before, even in the worst battles of the Western

Desert, had Farran's men experienced such an intensive and ferocious attack. When the last of the dive bombers made off, the fighters swung in at low level, machine-gunning anything and everything; it was a horrific, bloody nightmare.

The hail of machine-gun bullets lashed the olive trees and undergrowth, hammering into the men, women and children huddled in trenches below. 'It seemed aimless, senseless, but the purpose was clear,' said John Hetherington, a war correspondent then with the Australian Air Force. 'The German bombers and fighter pilots were trying to daze the defenders of Crete so that the way might be easier for the paratroops and glider-borne troops already flying across the Aegean.'

The scene afterwards was awesome.

> Soldiers, civilians, women, children, young and old lay bleeding and screaming amongst the already dead. Our three principal towns, Canea, Heraklion and Rethymo were bombed time and time again until not a wall was left standing, not one stone upon another. The wretched inhabitants, as they struggled to escape from their primitive shelters, were mercilessly butchered by fighter pilots deliberately swooping in at low level and the agony of these women and helpless little children left these raging beasts unmoved. Hospitals were smashed, wounded men finished off, and the orgy of destruction was complete.

Such were the carefully chosen words in the report of Greek Prime Minister, General Metaxas.[12]

Such were the hazards that Joanna Stavridi had chosen to face.

Just as suddenly as they had appeared on that morning of 20 May 1941, the bombers and fighters vanished. Overhead now was heard a different kind of noise, the drumming of old Junkers 52 engines. They were flying in slow formations of three. A tank officer looked up from his slit trench, swore incredulously and cried, 'The bastards are landing!'

In the sky were hundreds of green, red and yellow parachute canopies puffing open. 'Cripes!' shouted New Zealand Sergeant Templeton, stumbling over his mess tin as he stepped back to get a better view. He could not believe his eyes. 'Cripes, they can't be real? Surely they're dummies!'[13]

Sure enough, set against that azure blue Cretan sky and seen through a frame of grey-green olive branches they looked just like puppets, little dolls with arms and legs, jerking under colourful puffed-up skirts. Even Templeton's platoon commander, Lieutenant Thomas, did not want to believe what he saw. 'I struggled to grasp the meaning of this colourful fantasy, to realize that those beautiful kicking dolls meant a repetition of all the horrors we had known in Greece.'[14]

Indeed, this was no puppet show. 'They're parachutists, Sergeant,' he shouted, realizing that something was expected of him. 'Look at those planes. The next lot will fall right on us. Get ready for action!'

It was a fantastic scene. Parachutists were dropping everywhere in hundreds, falling straight down on to the villages and the vines, straight into the arms of the waiting men, on to tents, on to the slit trenches and the guns. The morning sky was filled with twisting, turning aircraft, hundreds of them bearing down in long lines from the sea. And swishing low overhead too were the ghost planes, planes that made no noise – gliders, huge aircraft heading directly for Maleme airfield. Rifles crackled, Bren guns 'brrrumped' in five-round bursts from olive trees as all the troops came into action. Bofors guns joined in with their steady sharp 'quacks' as the noise built up into a tremendous crescendo.

Thus began the biggest and bloodiest airborne operation of the whole war. So bloody a business was it that never again on the same scale would Germany repeat it.

For nearly two hours, they had dive-bombed and machine-gunned the hospital where Joanna Stavridi tended the wounded. 'Bullets ripped tents open and set some on fire. Patients who could walk sheltered in slit trenches, men who could not move had to lie in their cots while the strafing went on,' observed John Hetherington.[15]

As the first wave of parachutists began to float down, tank commander Roy Farran leapt to his feet, shouting, 'Open fire. Get the bastards.'[16] The cry was echoed from Canea to Maleme, from Suda Bay to Galatos as soldiers dashed into the open firing with any weapon they could lay their hands on. A New Zealand brigade band at early morning practice tossed away their instruments, seized rifles, and even used the bayonet shoulder to shoulder with the Maoris to beat off the attackers. Everyone was in the front line now. John Hetherington recalled how even a New Zealand concert party abandoned their make-up boxes and false wigs and proved they could fight as competently as they could sing and mime.

The rapid fire plucked at the swinging 'dolls' in the sky now screaming with fear and pain. 'It was just like a duck shoot,' said one South Islander from the 23rd New Zealand brigade. And its commanding officer, Colonel Leckie, in the first chaotic five minutes shot five German parachutists himself without even moving from his headquarters.

But still they came on relentlessly, many of the parachutists 'pre-medicated' with injections to give them abnormal stamina and to ward off fatigue.[17] (The British had not yet issued their infantry with 'wakey-wakey' pills.) Hundreds of parachutists dropped on Maleme airfield whilst it was still being swept by the defender's artillery, mortar and machine-gun fire. Still they kept dropping, squirming and making running motions with their legs to break the fall on landing. Bren gunner John Bennett recalled:

> The place was just like a abbatoir. This was easier than anything we had ever come across in training. We shot them as they hung entangled in the shroud lines looped on to olive trees, shot as they sprawled on the rock-hard ground with legs broken on landing. Anti-aircraft guns fired at the lumbering JU 52s and could not miss. I saw planes burst into flames, then the men inside feverishly leaping out. Some were burning as they dropped to earth.[18]

And tending to the mutilated bodies of both sides, under terrible conditions, was Joanna Stavridi, with the staff of the battered 97th General Hospital.

By the end of the day the Third German Parachute battalion had been virtually wiped out. Everyone who could handle a weapon had been in on the shoot. Brigadier Kippenberger recalled, 'I stalked one paratrooper round the side of a house and shot him cleanly through the head at ten yards.'[19]

That night, Prime Minister Churchill told the House of Commons that 'The greater part of the airborne invaders had been wiped out by dusk.' And bulletins from Middle East Headquarters talked of Germans being 'mopped up' and of the situation being 'under control' …

It did not seem at all under control to Joanna at the tented hospital. A battle was raging on all sides. At one point, German parachutists broke through British defences shouting a battle cry, '*Hoch! Hoch!*' and then made off elsewhere, leaving the hospital as it was. At another time a German section dashed into a ward brandishing machine pistols and shouting, '*Raus! Raus!*' No one took any notice of them and they too disappeared. It was a chaotic situation.

Clearly the optimism expressed in those first British news bulletins was grossly misplaced. True, German casualties were enormous but what Churchill and the compilers of the news bulletins had not known was the astonishing scale of the operation: 3,000 parachutists dropped in the first hour. These were progressively reinforced throughout the day by gliders, and later, when the Maleme airfield had been captured, by troop-carrying aircraft. Then came a steady stream of huge planes bringing in reinforcements, with no more interference than aircraft arriving at a civil aerodrome in peacetime. Soon, 22,000 crack German troops were deployed against the ill-equipped, battle-fatigued Allied troops.

The seriousness of the situation was perhaps most evident at Joanna's 97th General Hospital, situated in 'No Man's Land' between two strategic points.

In an attempt to relieve the pressure from this area, Brigadier Kippenberger called for tanks. Captain Roy Farran at that moment was pulling the crackling earphones off his head and rubbing his ears when he heard his code letter called. He settled himself on the small, saddle-like seat, listened for a few moments and then gave his orders. They were to cover the withdrawal of New Zealanders from the Maleme airfield.

As his tank advanced along a narrow village street, long files of New Zealand infantry stumbled past him. Their boots and gaiters were white with dust, their bleached drill shirts filthy, shapeless and torn, showing dark patches of sweat. And their faces, peeling scarlet or glistening brown, were blotched with ugly sores painted gentian violet, from which stubble bristled. They were a weary, worn-out lot. They trudged along as if in a trance in which all senses were anaesthetized. Ten paces between files, four paces between the men in each file. Along the road outside the village were the graves of the dead: some had merely a stick and a British helmet leaning drunkenly from it.

Farran had travelled about a mile down the road when there was a blinding flash inside the tank. The gunner sank groaning to the bottom of the turret. The driver too was wounded. A moment later, Farran also was hit in both legs and in his right arm. Somehow he managed to push the wounded gunner and driver out through the driver's hatch and then crawled out himself.[20]

Stretcher bearers took him to the casualty clearing station where 300 wounded sprawled, tormented by flies. 'From there I was humped over the hill by four stretcher bearers to the 97th General Hospital. I spent the night there under the tender care of a British woman dressed in a shirt and battledress. Her presence on the island was a complete mystery to me.'

That woman, of course, was Joanna Stavridi and in the next few days, her resourcefulness, stamina and audacity would earn her the admiration of Allies and Germans alike and bring her the highest award for valour for her nursing service.

Soon the hospital was overwhelmed with casualties as attack and counter-attack raged around the tented wounded, with New Zealanders and crack German parachutists battling for possession. Anyone who could move, made for the slit trenches. Any movement from there was followed by sniping bullets. It was an untenable situation.

Under the cover of darkness patients, who included German parachutists, were moved to the safety of caves nearer the sea shore, lately occupied by goats; there were three caves for the patients and a small one for the doctors and operating theatre.

The next day 500 more casualties poured in, many of whom were beyond human aid. The operating table was towards the mouth of the cave to make the most of daylight but the cave floor sloped, it was fouled with goat excrement, and doctors slipped and stumbled over amputated limbs. Amongst a welter of blood and stench, Joanna, who had once written home during her training to say that she wondered whether the smell of ether and the sight of wounds would make her sick, found that she had no time even to think about the conditions under which they were working.

Battles were being waged almost on their doorstep, haste and improvisation were the order of the day. Bandages could not be changed, a pungent odour of rotting flesh filled the air, some of the men had dysentery and lack of facilities for disposing of human excrement added to the stench. Men rolled on to their sides from the stretchers to urinate into a ration can brought round by an orderly. Another walked round dispensing the Army's panacea, hot tea lavishly thickened with sweetened, condensed tinned milk.

Doctors, orderlies and Joanna as theatre nurse dealt with ghastly cases: young men looking terribly old for their years, mouths tight drawn, men who had known the bitter sorrow of seeing their friends blasted beyond recognition. It was no wonder that under such conditions doctors and nurses lost all sense of personal safety. Joanna was no exception.

Typical of her disregard of danger was her conduct when food became desperately short. Something had to be done. She had an idea. The swastika flag! German troops had run it up the hospital flagpole and then an orderly had pulled it down a few hours later and replaced it with the Red Cross flag. The swastika he had stuffed into his big pack as a souvenir. Now he was going to lose it.

Joanna borrowed it. Then with it rolled under her arm and a few heavy rocks in her hands she dashed out of the cave and spread the flag out over the ground, weighting it down with rocks: a signal to aircraft for help. That afternoon a German plane dropped food. Joanna's ingenuity and courage had paid dividends.[21]

One might wonder what it was that sustained her during all these trials. What was it that nourished her mental and physical strength during her ordeal as the sole woman nurse responsible for the badly wounded under bombardment and machine-gun fire? A clue to what it was that impelled her to keep going can be found in a letter home written earlier in the Greek campaign. In that letter she said:

> It's real *hate* I feel this time as they, the Germans, have not done a single action in this war which was not below the imagination of the average human being in beastliness and in any other words you would have to fill in for yourself, Daddy, though I fear you, Daddy, darling gentle thing, haven't got anything in your vocabulary bad enough.[22]

Time was incalculable during the height of the German onslaught upon the island. Inside the caves it was horrendous, outside hazardous as a continuous archway of shells sped low overhead with angry baleful screams to tear into the ground yards in front of the caves, bursting with a mighty crash. Close overhead too, machine-gun fire crackled.

All movement beyond the mouth of the caves had to be done at night. 'Even a corpse laid out to await burial by night was machine-gunned,' reported Anthony Cotterell.[23] Going from one cave to the next, staff had to flatten themselves against the cliff's face.

One night, by the light of a hurricane lamp, Joanna had some of her patients sew red crosses on to sheets so that the caves could be clearly marked. After these had been laid out by night the caves were no longer attacked by the Luftwaffe who respected the flag. But shells and mortar bombs still fell all round.

On Thursday 22 May 1941, the Anzacs knew they could no longer hold the crack German troops. The hospital got its orders to retire. It was to be evacuated at 2300 hours and personnel were to move inland with walking wounded to the small village of Neochorio. They would be accompanied by a military escort.

When the escorting troops arrived the officer in charge stressed the fact that at this time only the walking wounded were to be taken. Joanna asked what was to become of the seriously disabled men. She was told that trucks would be sent for them at three o'clock in the morning.

'Then,' said Joanna, 'I shall stay with those who need me most.'

The main party set off in their retreat, displaying large Red Cross flags, and carrying minimum equipment as they made their way over the rough country towards the south of the island. 'Tin hats had to be used as drinking cups, wash-basins, and bed-pans, and six-inch nails taken out of walls made practical orthopaedic appliances,' wrote Cotterell.[24]

Back in the caves Joanna ministered to the badly wounded, waiting, preparing for the moment when, in the small hours of the morning, the trucks would come for the remainder of the wounded. Then there would be no time to spare at all. All must be ready.

Three o'clock came and went. No trucks. Dawn broke. A makeshift breakfast was eaten. Still no signs of transport. They waited. Soldiers made the usual wan little jokes. No one was deceived. It was all part of a play they had acted so many times before. Everyone knew what the others were feeling. And as the afternoon wore on the uppermost thought was, 'Oh Christ. So this is it. There'll be no bloody trucks.'

Towards evening news came. A truck had arrived! A truck? One truck. A lieutenant got out and gave orders. Rear party of orderlies and Joanna were to get aboard.

'But what about the badly wounded?' asked Joanna. 'What's to happen to them?'

A helpless shrug of the escort officer's shoulders came with his reply, 'They will be left.'

Joanna stared blankly, not moving. The choice was clear: to

save herself by leaving on the truck or to stay with the wounded and be captured by the Germans. She wasted no time. Her mind was made up. She turned to the officer and said, 'Then I shall stay with them.'[25]

What happened next is history. On 26 May 1941, the British commander on the island, General Freyberg, reported: 'In my opinion the limit of endurance has been reached by troops under my command ... our position is hopeless.'

Thus it all came to a sad and inevitable end. He withdrew his gallant army southwards, hammered all the way by dive bombers and fighting patrols as the Germans tried to turn an orderly withdrawal into a rout. Men staggering along half asleep, their knees weak, sank heavily to the ground for the ten-minute break each hour and slept where they lay for a few minutes and then heaved themselves to their feet, shouldered their rifles and plodded onwards. Propelling them for those last few miles was that special reserve of strength, the instinct for survival that seems to rise to the aid of mankind when most needed and becomes a powerful driving force.

At last they arrived. A cordon of heavily armed infantry was thrown around the beaches and the evacuation of the Allied Force by the Royal Navy began on 28 May 1941. It ended on 31 May. Of the 27,550 men sent to Crete, 14,850 came back, 1,800 had been killed and 10,900 taken prisoner. Amongst these prisoners at first was Joanna Stavridi.

Soon after the last of the British trucks had left her with the wounded, German armoured vehicles came thundering down the road towards the temporary hospital in the caves. A German staff car drew up, two officers got out and could scarcely believe their eyes when they found a woman there amongst the shell holes and bullet-pitted rocks. But it was not a British nurse they saw. Not any longer.

Joanna Stavridi had hastily donned her Greek Red Cross nurse's uniform. The Germans were impressed by the efficient manner in which she went about her duties; impressed and somewhat amused too by the way this young nurse swore in the lurid vernacular of Greek soldiers when orderlies were slow in getting things done. She seemed too good to be left in Crete. They put her on a plane and flew her to Athens to work in a hospital in Petraki.

The 'Florence Nightingale of Crete', the British press called her later when details of the cool way she had accepted danger and the possibility of death became known from survivors' reports. She was, in August 1941, awarded the highest honour for valour of the Hellenic Red Cross. It was a fitting tribute to a heroine whose courage and endurance had been stretched to the utmost capacity in the twelve days of what a Cairo communiqué described as 'the fiercest fighting of this war'.

Joanna Stavridi, without doubt, was made in the mould of the true hero or heroine who knows the abyss of fear yet does not hesitate to walk along its edge.

5

Survivor Against the Odds

I was near the end of the line on the right. We waded
into the surf and were almost up to our waists in the
water when they just fired on us from behind. I don't
think anybody screamed. We weren't even
frightened. There was no panic, no hysteria, no tears.
We just accepted it as being our lot.

Staff Nurse Vivien Bullwinkel

Heroines, in wartime, as we have already seen, appear to have
a philosophy of life that gives them a natural acceptance of the
inevitable, an attitude that fortifies them against fear. It is such
an attitude too, which enables them to take risks and cope with
situations with complete disregard for their own safety.

Nowhere is this point illustrated better, I think, than in the
heroism of those Australian and British nursing sisters
captured by the Japanese after the fall of Singapore in February
1942. Sadly, many of them did not survive the horrific ordeals
and callous treatment. There were many amongst these
unfortunate young women who were heroines in their own
right. And from amongst the survivors it might seem invidious
to single out any one for special mention. But by following the
personal experience of one of these young women we can
perhaps appreciate more vividly those qualities which make a
heroine, qualities which even today, nearly half a century later,
are an inspiration to others. The story of Sister Margot Turner,
of the Queen Alexandra's Imperial Military Nursing Service, is
in this category.

In the spring of 1941, Sister Margot Turner was twenty-nine
and enjoying life to the full in the Indian hospital at Meerut, not
far from Delhi, which was famous for its role in the Indian
Mutiny. She was a tall, well-built, attractive woman with brown
wavy hair beneath her crisply starched hospital cap. She had

what her friends described as 'a good face, with candid blue eyes and a mouth that often seemed to have the suggestion of a smile about to break forth'. The image she projected was that of a woman to be reckoned with – a woman dedicated to her job yet one who could revel in her leisure activities off-duty.

She had trained for four years under the strict discipline of St Bartholomew's, London, with long working hours of 6.30 a.m. to 6 p.m., and only one day off a month, yet still managed to keep up with her sport – swimming, hockey and tennis – as well as fitting in time for riding the Life Guards' horses at Knightsbridge. All this took some organizing in those days when nurses worked twelve hours a day and had to be in bed with lights out at 10.30. But then Margot Turner was like that; she could accept a situation and build her life around it.

She had been posted to India in 1939 and in Meerut Hospital was a highly regarded theatre sister, though like most young nurses, she was at various times awed and fascinated, intrigued and repulsed by what she witnessed. She had grown used to seeing death but still found it emotionally disturbing. However, she had developed her own way of coping with the stress of her demanding job and found vigorous physical activity to be an effective antidote to stress, a reassuring balm. And, as Margot was a popular young woman, she joined in whatever sports and games were currently being organized. No wonder she was fit and tough.

Life at Meerut's British garrison hospital was certainly very enjoyable – and not least for the nursing sisters. There were plenty of young men who were only too eager to escort them to dances, to films in the open-air cinema, and to take them on picnics at the weekend. If any of these young escorts were not available at weekends because of duty commitments then they would readily lend nurses their horses and their cars. One could, there, lead a very congenial life.

But it was no longer altogether satisfactory for Margot Turner. She felt uneasy with such a life of luxury with the war going so badly for Britain then.

By 1941 she had seen news reels showing the defeat of the British Expeditionary Force in France and the bombing of London, and reading between the lines of newspaper reports she realized that the war news on every front – the Atlantic, North Africa and the Mediterranean – was depressing for the Allies. The loss of Crete in May 1941 after a battle of only a few days appeared as a crowning disaster in a succession of setbacks and added much to the growing reputation of German invincibility. Now Hitler, with his southern flank secured by his victories in Greece and Crete, had turned his attention to the Soviet Union and his armies were already racing across the broad Russian Steppes towards Moscow and Kiev.

Thus, to Sister Turner, it seemed that Germany was winning every campaign. And she began to feel increasingly restless. It did not seem right to her that when so many men and women were making sacrifices for the war effort, she should be having such a comfortable life, and so she began submitting one application after another for a posting to active service in Europe.

She was impelled by something more than a passing desire or a feeling of patriotism; it was an urge to do what she considered to be 'the right thing'. Each month the response of her superiors to those applications was always the same, negative. Owing to the exigences of the Service ... etc. ... etc. she could not be spared. The truth was she was too good at her job and the surgeons were reluctant to release her, but in the end she got her way. At least she thought she had, when a posting order came for her to report to the transit camp in Bombay for onward despatch.

When the details of her destination came through she found that she was not going to Europe at all, as she had requested, but to the number 17 Combined General Hospital, Kuala Lumpur, situated about a third of the way up the Malay Peninsular. An even quieter backwater, it seemed.

When she arrived there, Margot Turner was put in charge of the operating theatre. Life for her was so frustrating that she wrote to her mother in a fit of anger, saying: 'We are supposed to be on active service but I have never been so inactive in all my life!' She had time on her hands for leisurely rounds of golf, for long afternoon walks and for parties in the mess and club at night. For the expatriates in Malaya then business was booming, rubber and tin were fetching high prices on the world market and there was a curious air of prosperity and optimism. Those late autumn days of 1941 were idyllic and the war news from Britain, though increasingly alarming, seemed, in peaceful Malaya, as remote as the moon.

Some of the more far-sighted of those expatriates, however, were aware of the growing peril surrounding them. They spoke in whispers of the Japanese threat which appeared more alarming since the collapse of France in 1940; its colony of

French Indo-China had been handed over to Japan, leaving merely a defenceless Siam standing between the British Army and the Japanese. Clearly, an invasion of Malayan territory could be considered a possibility. But then, the prosperous Brits were reassured by reports of British troops arriving to man the northern outposts and everyone knew that one British soldier was worth four Japanese. And so even amongst the most pessimistic of the gloom and doom brigade it seemed that nothing would be likely to upset their prosperity and security. Had they not been assured by the Malayan High Command that the jungle to the north was impenetrable? And so they carried on enjoying their own private Indian summer. Every night the streets of Singapore were full of men and women going out to night clubs where tuxedo-clad men and bare-shouldered women drifted together around the dance floor.

The events at dawn on 7 December 1941 put an end to all that, and the radio news of them that morning struck the world like a thunderclap. Shortly before sunrise and ahead of any declaration of war, 350 Japanese bombers delivered a shattering attack upon the United States fleet riding proudly at anchor at the sleeping Hawaiian island base of Pearl Harbor. That mighty fleet, which had boasted mastery of the Pacific, was now a mass of blackened, twisted metal. In little over an hour the Japanese had gained control of the Pacific.

Almost simultaneously with the air attack upon Pearl Harbor Japanese assault troops attacked the morthern Malay Peninsula, Hong Kong and the Philippine island of Luzon, north of Manila. Hordes of small men wearing light equipment and cloven shoes to facilitate climbing up trees in jungle warfare were now taking on the crack troops of the American and British armies. Firing their German-pattern tommy guns from the hip, they made phenomenally rapid progress. Japan's might now seemed to overshadow the whole of the Far East. Never before had a nation started a war with such colossal victories.

At breakfast time on 8 December, Singapore Radio announced that the United States, Britain and the Commonwealth and China were now at war with Japan. Only then did the ex-patriates in Malaya and millions of Americans back in the States wake up to a world of reality, stripped of romance and sentiment. That night, when nurses and troops in Singapore were trying to come to terms with the fearsome news, they heard a frightening roar growing louder and louder. They looked up and saw streams of tracer bullets streaking through the black sky. Singapore was being bombed. Further north, bombs were falling around the hospital at Kuala Lumpur. Now, at last, Margot Turner really was 'on active service'. Now she would be able to do the job for which she had been so well trained.

Everything then happened so quickly that events seemed to merge into one long nightmare. Kuala Lumpur was bombed and the hospital immediately evacuated to Singapore where it joined forces with the Alexandra Hospital. Swiftly wards and corridors were filled with the mutilated bodies of battle casualties. Margot worked non-stop, snatching a few hours' sleep in cat naps until towards the end of January 1942 when Singapore garrison itself was threatened by the advancing Japanese army. Ahead of it came sickening news of the atrocities already committed by its more barbaric soldiers in Hong Kong. There, on Christmas morning, they had burst into St Stephen's College Emergency Hospital, bayoneted the two senior doctors who had rushed to meet them displaying the flag of the Red Cross, ripped bandages off the wounded in bed and bayoneted them too, and then taken off the nurses to be repeatedly raped. Three of them they killed as well. When the news of this savagery reached General Percival at Malayan Command Headquarters he ordered all Allied nurses to be compulsorily evacuated.

It was at tea time on 13 February, amidst much confusion, that hospital nurses were parted from their patients and after being assembled together at the Singapore Cricket Club, transported through the devastated dockyard to a quayside where a launch waited to take them to a small ship called the *Kuala*. Already it was packed beyond its safety capacity with 400 women and children, 300 servicemen and a group of other nurses with four hospital matrons.

'There was an air raid whilst we were trying to get on board,' recalled one nursing sister. 'Planes dived low and machine-gunned the little launch. Sisters were killed from this and from bomb splinters on the boat itself. Once we all got aboard there was standing room only.'[1]

All over the dockyard now flames leapt from burning buildings and warehouses on the waterfront into the murky twilight sky. On the outskirts of the city Union Jacks were being hauled down, to give pride of place to the treacherous emblem of the Rising Sun. And when darkness fell the _Kuala_ eased its way out of the harbour, steaming through the night between the small islands scattered about those seas. At dawn the captain anchored the ship about a quarter of a mile off one of those islands, thinking it would be safer to keep off the high seas until it was dark again. But at 7 a.m. a Japanese reconnaissance plane came over and was soon followed by a flight of six bombers. Then it was that the captain of the ship issued a rather strange order to all nursing sisters: 'Get out of your white dresses and overalls and into something less conspicuous.' Margot borrowed a grey dress and hurriedly changed into it whilst all around was the deafening din of battle. The four hospital matrons had gathered for a conference when the ship got a direct hit. The bomb fell through the captain's bridge, down to the boiler room bursting the boilers and setting the ship on fire. All four matrons were killed. 'We had three raids on the ship and they came over four times while we were swimming in the sea and dive-bombed and machine-gunned us,' wrote one of the nursing sisters.[2] The death toll in the sea was enormous as there were only two life-boats and insufficient life-belts to go round. The nearest island was at least a quarter of a mile away and there was a very swift current which kept throwing everyone back to the ship. Eventually Margot Turner and others landed on the island of Pompong.

Nurses evacuated from Singapore in other ships that same day fared no better. Those on the _Empire Star_ were repeatedly dive-bombed, attacked by torpedoes and machine-gunned before the ship sank. During one such raid, Staff Nurses Margaret Anderson and Veronica Torney were caught on deck tending to the wounded. They continued to nurse and lay across their patients to protect them when the planes dived to strafe the ship with machine-gun fire. Anderson received the George Medal and Torney the MBE for their bravery.[3]

Other nurses sailing on the _Vyner Brooke_ on the same day fared even worse. When their ship was sunk, nurses in life-jackets were carried for sixteen hours in the strong currents before reaching an island shore. Twenty-two Australian Army nurses who landed from a life-boat on Banka Island suffered the worst fate.

They were still wearing their Red Cross arm bands and had barely recovered from their ordeal of being shipwrecked when twenty Japanese soldiers arrived and gave orders for all the men to stand on one side and the women to assemble at the other. This done, the men were marched away out of sight behind a promontory. A few minutes later there was a sound of gunfire and muffled screams, then the Japanese soldiers returned wiping blood off their bayonets. Now it was the turn of the women.

They too were formed into a line but this time they were ordered to march down the beach and into the sea. They all knew what to expect. Proudly, heads erect, chins up, they marched ahead into the lapping wavelets, ankle deep, then knee deep and were still going forward as the sea lapped their waists when Japanese machine guns opened fire on them from behind. Sister Vivien Bullwinkel was more fortunate than any of the others. A bullet hit her in the loin, throwing her face down in the water where she remained floating, feigning death. Gradually, gently turning her head sideways to breathe and with imperceptible movements of her hands, she drifted into a jungle creek where she crawled ashore and hid in the undergrowth. From her lair she watched the section of Japanese soldiers form up and march away. Of the twenty-one other nurses not one survived the massacre.[4]

Meanwhile, on the small island of Pompong, Margot Turner lay recovering from her struggle to swim against the current. She did not have long to rest for there was a shout and more excitement. Another ship, the *Tanjong Penang*, had put into the harbour. It too, was full of women and children, wounded servicemen and survivors picked up from the scores of other wrecks. The *Tanjong*'s captain asked for volunteers from nurses to go aboard his ship to nurse the wounded. It was not an easy decision for any of those nurses to make. They had seen so many ships sunk by the Japanese Air Force and Navy. Surely it would be safer to stay on dry land, even as a prisoner, than to risk suffering another shipwreck?

Nevertheless, Margot and others volunteered without hesitation and that night sailed on the *Tanjong Penang*. Margot was at work from the moment her feet touched the deck, moving amongst the wounded, changing dressings and giving encouragement to those packed in the foetid hold.[5]

Some hours later, long after sunset, she and her companions climbed up to the deck and lay down to breathe the fresh air. They were just drifting into a well-earned sleep when they were suddenly awakened by the bright beam of a searchlight blazing at them from close quarters. Almost immediately there followed a series of ear-splitting explosions as the guns of a Japanese warship opened fire. Shells tore through the thin steel plates of the cargo ship. 'I was lying next to Sister Beatrice le Blanc,' recalled Margot Turner, 'and there were people dead and dying all around us. Beatrice got a nasty wound in the buttock which she said nothing about at the time. The ship was a ghastly shambles of mutilated bodies.'[6]

Down below, where the women and children were packed, the scene was indescribable. One nurse who managed to scramble up to the deck arrived with her dress drenched in blood and told how the hold of the ship had received the full force of one of the shells and was absolutely smashed, with bodies pulped. By this time the ship had canted over at a steep angle and quivered on the brink of turning over. 'Beatrice and I just stepped into the sea and were very lucky not to be sucked down when the ship suddenly turned over and sank,' recalled Margot Turner. Thus for the second time in three days, they were shipwrecked.

Margot Turner's ordeal had been bad enough already but worse was to come. In the few minutes before the ship disappeared beneath the Java Sea, the officers had managed to throw a few small rafts overboard. Beatrice and Margot got hold of two which they tied together. Amongst the dead bodies and debris floating in the darkness were women and children screaming and dying from their wounds. Margot and Beatrice swam around the two rafts picking up as many people as they could and guiding them to the rope handles at the side of the floats. Altogether they brought in fourteen people, including children. These two rafts were so small that only two people could sit on one raft at a time. Margot organized it so that four women sat in pairs, back to back, each holding a child on their knees. All the others were in the water with Margot swimming round keeping them awake and reminding them not to let go of the rope handles whatever the reason or the current would carry them away. Despite her efforts, two of the fourteen were gone when dawn broke. With her in the water was Beatrice, ministering to all the others despite the ugly open wound in her buttock through which she lost blood. That afternoon, Margot became alarmed at her friend's condition. From the ashen colour of her face it was clear that Beatrice was failing rapidly. Margot was a strong swimmer but it took all her strength to heave her friend up on to the raft. There Margot was shocked to see the deep gaping wound, raw flesh still oozing blood. Clearly, unless they were picked up soon she would die. Never once, though, did Beatrice complain. She lay, her parched body now encrusted with sores, facing death as she had faced life, unflinchingly. Towards the middle of that afternoon, when Margot was holding her head, Beatrice moved her cracked and swollen lips into the semblance of a smile and then just seemed to fall asleep. Not long afterwards she stopped breathing and died.

Sister Turner said a brief prayer and gently lowered her friend's body into the water.

Now the blazing tropical sun reflected from the water was beginning to take its toll; angry, open salt-water sores appeared on parched shoulders and necks, pus-filled boils bulged under flaking skin, tongues became hard and dry. Morale evaporated like water splashes on the raft, minds began to cloud over and gradually the weaker and wounded ones were robbed of their will to live. Towards evening two more women relinquished their hold on the life lines and slid beneath the surface, never to reappear. Others became delirious, gabbling and mumbling through their swollen, distorted mouths. 'By the end of the second day all six children went mad,' recalled Margot. 'We had a terrible time with them.'[7] Soon every one of them died and Margot carefully examined each one to make sure they really were beyond any further help, thinking all the time that somewhere some mother might be grieving for the lost child. When she was absolutely sure they were dead, Margot committed them to the deep with a prayer, for she was a deeply religious woman.

Perhaps it was her faith as well as her strong physical constitution which contributed to her endurance and to her determination to cling on to life when others gave in. By the end of that terrible burning hot day of 19 February 1942, and the evening that followed, there was only one other woman left with her. They both climbed on to the raft and huddled back to back, their legs dangling in the shark-infested water. With voices that were hoarse and weak, and through misshapen mouths, they introduced themselves to each other. Sister Margot Turner's sole companion on the raft was Mrs Barnett.

In the ghostly light of dawn the next day, as far as the eye could see, there was not another living soul as the little raft drifted at the mercy of the strong Java Sea currents. They decided to release the second raft, thinking one would be more manageable. Both women were still mentally strong enough to have some hope of rescue even though there appeared to be no sign of aircraft or shipping. Later that afternoon however, they realized that they were drifting between small islands, though not near enough to reach them by swimming. Swirling around them were odd bits of timber and driftwood. Margot caught hold of one piece and found that she could make some impression upon the raft's direction by using the wood as a makeshift paddle.

Mrs Barnett then managed to grab a piece of wood and she too began to paddle. Speaking only when necessary they directed the small raft towards one of the islands. Now there seemed to be more hope that they might just reach one of them and find water. In the intense heat of the day physical effort was extremely unpleasant. Their pores had closed up during the first two days and they no longer perspired, their body temperature seemed to rise even more, their hands, never before hardened with such work and softened further by immersion in salty sea water, soon became blistered. Skin peeled from their palms, leaving raw flesh beneath. their nails became brittle and broke easily and cuticles peeled away. Added to all that discomfort their backs ached almost unbearably from sitting in the crouched position in which they were trying to exert pressure on their makeshift paddles.

Nevertheless, they seemed to be making some progress until Mrs Barnett's paddle slipped from her hand. She reached out for it, missed and then suddenly turned, grabbed a life-jacket and slipped into the water, swimming towards the drifting wood despite Sister Turner's weak shout telling her not to go from the raft. The current was far too strong for Mrs Barnett's enfeebled limbs to cope with. All too quickly she was swept away and disappeared from sight.

Now Margot was alone. It was no use now for her to attempt to paddle. She lay down to conserve her strength, and prayed. In wartime there were many who turned to God when the situation was desperate, even though that God for them had always seemed as uncertain and remote as infinity in mathematics. But for Margot Turner, God was real enough and could help. Patiently she lay, accepting her situation for what it was, and waited.

At times she became light-headed, dozed lightly and dreamed of ice-cold drinks, of fruit and cups of tea in the sisters' mess. The raft, now with a solitary motionless figure on board, was merely a white speck upon the mirror-like surface of the Java Sea. There was little chance of it being spotted by any passing aircraft or ship. Death for Margot Turner was near. Her parched throat craved for a drink, her body was burnt mahogany brown, but not once did she countenance the thought that she would die. On the contrary, though she accepted the fact that her situation was desperate, she refused to give in. She would fight with Fate which had placed her in this grim position. She was determined it should not beat her into submission.

That night it rained. A fine rain. She held back her head and put out her tongue, trying to catch a few drops. Then she remembered that still in the pocket of her tattered grey dress was her small powder compact. She opened it out and caught a few drops of rainwater in that too. She sucked the rain-soaked cloth of her dress and ate some seaweed that floated past the raft. Then purposefully, she turned her mind to happier times. She thought of home and of her loved ones. She knew from all her nursing experience that if she showed too much anxiety for those patients she was nursing they would worry too, lose heart, despair and die. Now that she was nursing herself she applied those same principles, husbanding all her resources and making sure that she kept an alert and positive attitude to the situation. The gravest danger she knew lay in letting go, falling into a deep sleep or even a coma and then slipping off the raft to her death. Again she prayed and made herself recall names of places and people she had met in various hospitals to keep herself awake. And so the spark of life was kept aglow.

On the afternoon of the fourth day, Margot Turner was in the last stages of physical exhaustion. Her eyes were glazed when she looked around the horizon but then she jerked herself alert and peered across the glassy sea. Was it a ship or a mirage, a product of imagination, her wishful thinking? It was a ship.

She had no strength left to stand up and wave but she sat more upright and feebly waved an arm, showing that she was at least alive. The ship altered course and approached quite swiftly. It was a warship but as it came closer Margot's heart sank. Now she could see slit almond eyes in the yellow faces of the little men leaning over the rail. It was a Japanese ship. Jubilation gave way to despair. Perhaps, though, with her brown body, they would take her for a Malayan woman.

They threw a rope down to her and with gestures and shouts told her to tie it round her waist. She tried but failed. A sailor climbed down a rope ladder, tied the rope to her emaciated, shrivelled body, and, more dead than alive, she was hauled up over the rail on to the deck.

She feared the worst as she looked up at those perspiring Japanese faces peering down upon her. But in a strange way those ultimate, importuning prayers on the raft had been answered. A sharp order dispersed the ring of onlookers and an officer wearing steel-rimmed glasses appeared and knelt down by her blackened, dehydrated body. He touched her lightly, examined her closely and then stood up and gave a brusque order. There was a scurrying of feet as sailors ran to her side with a stretcher, lifted her gently and moved her into the shade of a deck awning. Now the destroyer was steaming steadily forward and a cooling breeze played over Sister Turner's prostrate body.

The Japanese doctor appeared again a few moments later with a bowl and a white napkin. He squatted down by her side, lifted her head and put the bowl of tea fortified with a little whisky to her lips. He let her take only a few sips. Then he lowered her down to rest for a while. Shortly afterwards he came again, this time bringing a bowl of milk and fed Margot a little at a time, all the while, reassuringly, saying a few words in English. He had been trained in an American medical school before the war and spoke good English. He found from his questions that she was a British nursing sister and from then on gave her his undivided attention, noting her reactions and modifying her fluid and food intake accordingly. A nursing orderly dressed her painful sores and sunburn.

When she was strong enough he had a clean shirt and trousers brought to her so that she could get out of the rough salt-soaked dress that was chafing her skin.

So concerned was the Japanese doctor with her welfare that even when the destroyer docked in the port of Muntok on the Dutch East Indies island of Banka, off Sumatra, it was the doctor himself and one of the sailors who carried her off the ship and on to the pier. After that it seemed he could do no more. His kindness had surely saved her life. He was of the same race as those who had ravaged the Hong Kong hospital and massacred the nurses on Banka. Perhaps his kindness went some way to redress those barbaric crimes against humanity.

As Margot Turner lay that day on the pier she was suddenly aware of voices calling to her in English. A group of British prisoners of war gathered round her and offered her food. She was just able to take a mouthful of peach but no more before the Japanese doctor ordered the men away and back to their work. He then lifted Margot and carried her himself down to the civilian prisoners' camp. There he handed her over to a nursing sister, saluted courteously and walked back to his ship.

Sister Briggs, who was on duty then, remembered Margot Turner's arrival. 'She was burnt black by the sun, her eyes sunk deep into her head. Until she spoke I had no idea she was English.'[8]

Curiously, the Japanese doctor had not yet altogether abandoned Margot Turner. During the four days that his ship was berthed in Muntok taking on provisions he visited Margot every day, to make sure that her recovery was progressing. Then, on the fourth day he arrived with a neat little parcel for Margot. It was her grey dress, cleaned, pressed and folded upon a hanger!

It was his parting gift. Now Margot Turner would have to recover on her own to face a long and terrible ordeal in prison.

The prison itself comprised eight huts with concrete floors surrounding an open square. The camp, built originally to house 200 Chinese coolies, now held 700 prisoners. Amongst them were Australian Army nursing sisters and some British civilian nurses who gradually filled in the gaps in the story of events which they had experienced since the fall of Singapore. All of them had horror stories to relate, of being bombed, machine-gunned, and shipwrecked. Into the camp one day walked Sister Vivien Bullwinkel, the sole survivor of the massacre of the twenty-two Australian Army nursing sisters on Banka Island. After hiding in the undergrowth for several days following the shooting, she found that the natives were too frightened of the Japanese to help her with food and so, in desperation, she gave herself up to a Japanese naval officer who took her in his car to the prison at Muntok. There she never again mentioned the massacre because she felt that her life might be in danger from those wishing to remove all evidence of the barbaric act. As it was, it was difficult enough to survive at all in that prison.

The diet there bordered on starvation and it said much for the toughness of Margot's constitution that she was able to make any recovery at all. Prisoners received two grey, watery helpings of rice each day with occasionally a few tough pieces of octopus tentacles. Two weeks after arriving at the prison, Margot suffered a setback. Ugly red, painful patches appeared on her legs and spread upwards towards the lymph glands of the groin. Sleep was impossible. The application of calamine recommended by the camp's Japanese medical officer had no therapeutic effect whatsoever. Steadily the condition deteriorated and Margot lapsed into a lethargic heap upon her straw mattress, until her friend in desperation managed to seek out an elderly Scotsman who had been practising medicine in Singapore. He diagnosed Margot's condition at once. There was no time to lose. The whole of her bodily systems were being poisoned by the pus from deep-seated, sea-water boils in both legs. He would have to operate. Margot recalled what happened. 'The boils had to be lanced at once and all we had to do it with was a blunt scalpel, and with this he opened up the red patches and out poured the pus.' Margot survived yet again. The kindly doctor died a few weeks later. The terrible conditions of that camp were just too much for his ageing constitution.

Not only was the camp overcrowded but the unhygienic conditions were appalling. Prisoners slept on the bare concrete floor except for the occasional turn on the one straw mattress provided for those in a weakened condition. A full night's sleep was never possible for regularly, throughout the hours of darkness, the Japanese guard patrol would rap the feet of prisoners with their torches as they passed, hit their legs with bayonets or flash the light in their faces. The stench was awful. Cut through the concrete were unprotected open drains which served as lavatories for both the Japanese and the prisoners. They were fly-infested and everyone suffered from infected mosquito or sandfly bites. Drinking water was limited to a mugful a day.

On 2 March many of the civilian men, women and children were moved across the Banka Straits to Palembang in Sumatra but someone had to stay behind in Muntok to look after the sick. Margot Turner was still amongst them and it was not until 1 April that she was anywhere near fit enough to be taken on a stretcher to Palembang. There, for yet another month she was nursed by Dutch nuns.

The chores of living behind barbed wire in Palembang camp were physically taxing; prisoners cooked their own meals on small smoky fires for which they had to find their own fuel, they took turns to carry heavy sacks of rice, their main diet, and in addition nurses like Margot Turner had also to look after the sick. On top of all these demands upon their physical endurance, they all had to cope with the Japanese habit of calling parades, a 'Tenko', at various times of the day and night. This meant standing out in the roadway, often in the hottest part of the day, in order to be counted by guards and officers. More often than not too, the counters would disagree on the total and there would be one recount after another until women were fainting and falling senseless. It was at one of these irritating Tenkos that Margot Turner did not bow low enough, as was demanded always, in front of one of the passing Japanese officers, who considered themselves lords of the earth; and for this omission she had her front tooth knocked out and lip smashed.

It was at this time that an unusual opportunity presented itself to Margot Turner.

Quite often in the Japanese camps volunteers were called for to work outside the camp but the 'work' was often of a dubious nature. Six nurses who went to scrub floors in houses in the city found themselves in the Red Light district and they were asked to sign a form saying, 'I am willing to entertain Japanese Officers', which they refused to do even though threatened with death. Another four nurses, recalled Nesta James, were informed that they would have to 'work' for the Japanese or starve.[9] They refused and their rations were cut so severely that they resorted to eating tapioca root which grew in one of the yards.

Fortunately, the pressure on the nurses to have Japanese as their 'friends' was removed when other women in the camp agreed to trade sex for favours. They abandoned all scruples for food and money to buy comforts for themselves and their children. And no one blamed them for making sacrifices for the sake of their children. Furthermore these 'Japanese girlfriends', or 'Jap bits' as they were generally known in the camps, became valuable sources of information about the state of the war and Japanese plans for the interned women. But even being a 'girlfriend' was a hazardous game. The Japanese had sudden changes of mind which brought violent reactions. It was far safer to be constantly vigilant and to volunteer for nothing and this was a policy which the Australian nurses agreed to adopt.

It was strange then, perhaps, to find Margot Turner, who had heard about the horrific experiences of others, volunteering to work outside the camp. Yet, in October 1942, Margot Turner, an inveterate volunteer, and three other nurses agreed, when asked by the Japanese commandant, to work in a native hospital run by Dutch and Indonesian doctors. They felt that at least they would be doing something useful instead of hanging about the internment camp being bored. Little did they think that their agreement would lead to an ordeal which only two of them would survive.

At first though, all went well. Margot was put in charge of the operating theatre and worked under an excellent Dutch surgeon. There was much to be done and in order to carry out her duties more efficiently, Margot learned to speak Malay. Occasionally, all four nurses were allowed to visit the local market to buy extra items of food and some special items for the patients. A rare treat. They were pleased that they had volunteered for the job. But suddenly, at the end of March 1943, a Japanese doctor was appointed to be in charge of the hospital and the Dutch doctor, for no particular reason, was thrown into prison. Discipline was tightened and relationships became inexplicably strained. On 6 April came a bolt from the blue. All four nurses were arrested and taken to prison. Without any explanation whatsoever they were put through the reception routine. Everything was taken from them – handbags, hairpins, glasses, rings, and even the elastic from their knickers. Hardly a word was spoken to them whilst this was going on, except when one of the prison officers said, 'Blue-eyed English. Ugh!' Their white muslin dresses were finally removed and they were each given white sarongs to wear. That seemed ominous – as if they were to stay for a long time.

From the reception room they were taken along a corridor on either side of which were small cells about twelve feet square. Each of the nurses was pushed into one of these small cells alongside murderers and thieves. From distant parts of the building came shrieks and groans.

'We were allowed out of the cell twice a day for about five minutes for exercise,' said Margot. 'The sanitary arrangements can be left to the imagination.' They were given two meagre meals a day either with cold tea or water, and forced to witness horrifying incidents of prisoners being tortured and executed. 'The things we saw were so horrible that I can't bear to think – much less talk – about them,' recalled Margot.[10] In that prison the two Dutch doctors died after their beatings.

Months went by. Still no reason was given for their imprisonment. The Japanese, in fact, seemed to have forgotten about their existence. They had no soap, nor a change of clothes, they were bitten by bugs, flies and fleas of all kinds in the hot, stuffy cells which lacked any real form of ventilation; and they had nothing in their slender diet to counteract disease. To survive under such conditions took a great strength of will. One of the nurses, Jennie, became ill with a form of typhoid fever. The four nurses were then moved into one slightly larger cell and Margot was able to nurse Jennie and persuade the guards to allow them a little more food. Life became one tedious effort to keep body and soul together.

To distract the others from their long hours of boredom and discomfort, Margot organized games to play in the cell, a form of draughts with the board being scratched on the floor with stones, and other pebbles used as the pieces. Stones were also used as chalk for competitions of noughts and crosses.

And so the days dragged by like a continuous nightmare. Nothing of what was happening elsewhere percolated into the putrid air of their cell. Here again, under such gruesome conditions, Margot's philosophy of accepting the situation and making the best of it, pulled them through. For, on 22 September 1943 and with no explanation whatsoever the four nurses were taken out of their foetid cells, bundled into a truck and sent to the women's interment camp now housed in vermin-infested huts. Australian Sister Betty Jeffrey remembered their arrival. 'They looked dreadful, their eyes had a wild look about them, they had lost a lot of weight but they were quite sane even if they did not look it. One of them had to go into the camp hospital where she later died.'[11]

Margot had barely recovered from her ordeal in prison when the women had to move camp again. By this time many of them were too weak and ill to undertake the terrible journey back to Palembang. They staggered along the long pier carrying and helping those too ill to walk. The guards packed them on to the deck of a small boat. During the next twenty-six hours as they sailed to Palembang, everyone was burnt black by the sun and eight women died. When they arrived at Palembang wharf the Japanese held another of the dreaded interminable Tenko parades. In their weakened state several other women fainted and died. Once the count was completed the women were packed into a train which then stood in a siding all night with all doors and windows securely closed. Before morning six more women died. The journey started at dawn. For three days and nights the women were kept cooped up in the heat. They were all nearly dead with weariness, thirst and hunger when they eventually arrived at their destination. Margot and her nursing colleagues were more weary than most as they had also to give what help they could to the sick. It was just before dawn on the fourth day that they were herded from the carriages by Japanese soldiers swinging their bayonets about the women's legs to hustle them along. By now several more had died.

At last they reached the camp, even more crowded and unhygienic than the last, with only twenty-two inches of bed space for each person on the floor. The terrible conditions and a diet lacking in protein and vitamins now gave rise to deficiency diseases. They lived on food that would barely have kept pigs alive: boiled banana leaves and cassava, which made them retch. Bones showed through the women's flesh, yet they looked fat with the swollen legs and the bloated 'rice-bellies' seen today in pictures of the starving in Africa.

Added to this condition, many of the nurses suffered also from neuritis of the hands and feet which they attributed to sleeping on cold concrete floors. Dysentery spread and on top of it all came an outbreak of beri-beri. Now, every day left a new corpse on the concrete. There was little or no ventilation and the air was putrid. Few women had energy enough to carry fuel or water for cooking and to make matters worse the 'Tenko' now took place twice a day to humiliate and punish internees, particularly the class-conscious British and the arrogant Dutch.

Naturally the nurses were vigilant as far as they could be about their personal hygiene; they had their hair cut short for ease and cleanliness. Many of them had ceased menstruating soon after their immersion in the sea, the shock of being shipwrecked and the ordeal of captivity, but others had to manage with cloth fragments until deprivation ended the problem. Leaves provided the only toilet paper.

In the last few months of captivity, the death rate escalated with the outbreak of a virulent new disease, Banka fever, a form of cerebral malaria, which left patients raving in delirium. At one time three-quarters of the camp, which comprised 700 inmates, was laid low with it.

Ironically, as the end of the war was so near, more and more of the women were dying. Sister Ellen Hannah wrote in her diary then:

I remained the sole surviving Sister of my Unit, (2/4th CCS), four were shot, two drowned, and two died in camp in 1945. One of these died a raving lunatic from cerebral malaria. I had begged the Commandant to give me anti-malarial medication, which they had withheld from Red Cross parcels; I was told there was plenty of room in the cemetery. He laughed, smacked my face and his guard hit me with his rifle.[12]

Suddenly, on 20 August everything changed. The prisoners were given fourteen pigs! It was the prison commandant's last-minute attempt to make up for past brutality. For the first time in years all prisoners had a satisfying meal, eating every edible part of those pigs, including ears and tails. What the prisoners did not know that day was that two weeks earlier, on 6 and 9 August 1945, the two atom bombs were dropped on Hiroshima and Nagasaki, killing 32,000 inhabitants.

The Japanese had been beaten back to their own shores, forced out of the territories they had occupied with such lightning speed nearly four years earlier. And now, when it was apparent Japan would have to surrender, signals from High Command ordered commandants of prison camps to destroy all evidence of the ill-treatment of prisoners of war. One extract alone provides striking testimony of the Japanese guilty knowledge. It reads: 'Personnel who ill-treated prisoners of war and internees, or who are held in extremely bad odour by them, are permitted to take care of the situation by immediately transferring or fleeing without trace.'[13]

Some senior commanders fled, others drew their swords and enacted the suicidal cult of hara-kiri to avoid a day of reckoning for the merciless tortures and unspeakable cruelties inflicted upon thousands of Allied prisoners of war and innocent civilians without compunction or compassion.

Now the liberators began searching for the prison and internment camps. During the second week of September 1945 a US aircraft flew over Margot Turner's camp, dropping fresh bread and medical supplies by parachute and then on 17 September an Australian plane landed to take off Australian Army nurses and very sick British. Twenty-four hours later another plane arrived to carry Margot Turner and her fellow prisoners to Singapore. Their ordeal of three years and seven months was over.

So ended a terrible time. The survivors of Japanese brutality and neglect had shown that women had the endurance and fortitude to come through unremitting emotional and physical hardship. Their story typified the bravery and courage of women in every land during the harrowing years of enemy occupation. Its human values were not restricted by differences of language. It was a story to which women of France and the Ukraine, the women of White Russia and the women of Greece and Crete, could relate.

6

The Soldier's Wife Who Fought Back

Claire Phillips has been praised by hundreds of ranking Army officers and prominent Filipino citizens for fortitude and courage which contributed materially to the success of the Philippine campaign. To this praise I wholeheartedly subscribe. It is an appropriate tribute for the brave, revenging wife of one of Bataan's fallen warriors.

Major John Peyton Boone, Infantry,
Army of the United States, Manila, 1946[1]

On Christmas Day 1941, 1,500 miles north-west from Singapore across the South China Sea, there stood a young woman, Claire, who felt gloriously happy despite her hazardous predicament. She was a strikingly handsome woman in her late twenties with great dark eyes, heavily lashed, and thick, curly, black hair framing an olive-skinned face which radiated good health. She was wearing well-washed clothes over a willowy body and looked decked out more for a camping holiday than for the serious ceremony about to take place. For in the middle of a battle she was about to be married.

Claire Phillips was standing at the edge of a wood some twenty miles south of Manila whilst artillery rumbled to the rear, and, not so far to the front, Japanese machine guns fired sporadic bursts. By her side stood a tall, brown-haired American soldier in combat dress, and forming a half circle on either side were a few of his friends. They were facing an improvised altar made of a fallen log covered with moss and wild flowers. From somewhere a bouquet of white hibiscus was pushed gently into her hands. All around, as if gracing the occasion, fluttered a myriad fireflies.

From a high spot behind the makeshift altar, Father Gonzales, a Filipino priest, was intoning, 'In nomine Patris et

117

Filii, et Spiritus Sancti ...' And suddenly it was all over. John
and Claire Phillips were man and wife. It had not been the big
family, Christmas wedding they had once talked about but it
was still a wedding and they had promised themselves to each
other till death did them part.

The reception was joyous but very simple. Packets of
sandwiches were unwrapped and mugs filled with lemon juice
and water spiked with US rum to toast the happy couple. All
too soon, John broke the bad news. He had to rush back to his
unit and patrol duty. Claire groped emotionally for words as
best she could; there was a catch in her voice with tears not far
away as she tried to put on a brave face. She had not expected
to be parted so quickly after the wedding ceremony.

For both John and Claire their romance had been a classic case
of love at first sight. It burgeoned rapidly from that first
meeting in Manila's Alcazar Club, where Claire earned enough
to support herself and small daughter Dian from her first
marriage which had gone disastrously wrong. Each night she
sang nostalgic songs to lonely US soldiers and Filipino citizens.

Claire noticed John the moment he came in with some of his
friends. 'I had never seen a more handsome man,' she later
recalled.[2] 'Over six feet of erect, well-proportioned he-man
with deep-set eyes under straight brows. And when I stepped
on the dais to sing, I sang – and I might as well confess it – to
him!' The choice was a sentimental song very popular in the
United States which she had left just a month previously,
typical of its time:

> I don't want to set the world on fire,
> I just want to start a flame in your heart.

Whilst she was singing this refrain their eyes met, held and
lingered as she went through the next part of the message of
love:

> In my heart I have but one desire
> And that is you, no other but you ...

Now, in that jungle clearing on the Philippines, her 'one
desire' had been fulfilled. But in the meantime the Japanese
had invaded the island of Luzon and Claire had fled from
Manila following her soldier fiancé, John, with scarcely time to

pack a few belongings. Now John was going back to a fighting unit in a division which was steadily withdrawing southwards.

For the first few days after the Japanese had launched their surprise attack, the outnumbered US forces and the poorly equipped Filipino troops had held the Japanese advance, but on 22 December the Commander of the Philippines, General MacArthur, had no alternative but to declare Manila an open city and withdraw his grossly outnumbered and unsupplied forces on Luzon to the Bataan Peninsula. Claire had travelled south too, keeping in close touch with her husband's unit. Nevertheless, it had still come as a great surprise when John had suddenly appeared on the afternoon of Christmas Day to tell her that everything was arranged for them to get married.

After the wedding Claire fled back to the hills with Dian, to hide from Japanese patrols searching for Americans for internment in the Santo Tomas camp in Manila. She could well imagine what perils a white American woman might have to face if she fell into those war-inflamed hands. But life in the hills where malaria was rife was far too dangerous for a young girl like Dian and so Claire sent her back to Manila with a Filipino family who were returning. They offered to smuggle her into the house of Judge Mamerto Roxas, a relative of John Phillips. John was now with General MacArthur's troops, who were packed into the narrow peninsula of Bataan which measured no more than twenty-five miles long by twenty wide. There the general's problem was not just with the advancing Japanese but with logistics – how to feed 100,000 servicemen and civilians. In that fever-stricken area most of his troops were soon laid low with malaria as well as being undernourished. Within a few weeks barely a quarter of them were fit enough to fight. Nevertheless, throughout January, February and March those few gallant men repulsed successive Japanese attacks aimed at driving them into the sea. By the middle of April 1942, however, greatly reinforced Japanese troops were thrown into the battle with massive artillery and air support, and the remnants of MacArthur's army were pushed right down to the end of the peninsula. Morale by this time was very low and General MacArthur had flown to a new base headquarters in Australia, promising he would be back. His deputy, General King, seeing no sign of relief coming, surrendered unconditionally to avoid mass slaughter.

Then began one of the most infamous chapters of Japanese military history. This was the notorious 'Death March' of

Bataan. Six days after the 76,000 starved, sick and exhausted Filipino and American troops surrendered they were herded into a column and ordered to march north in the oppressive, enervating heat of the tropical sun. Escorting the prisoners were the bestial troops of the savage Japanese 18th Division, already notorious for its pre-war atrocities in Nanking where a six-week orgy of murder, rape and pillage had left 200,000 Chinese dead. In the meantime the men had lost none of their brutality; they drove their prisoners, already weakened by lack of food and long weeks in the fighting lines, up the dusty, zig-zag hill roads from Marivales at the southern tip of the peninsula, sixty miles to the railway terminus at San Fernando.

Not surprisingly, as men sweltered in temperatures well over a hundred degrees fahrenheit, some fell out exhausted by the roadside where they were beaten with rifle butts and kicked until they tottered back into the column. Those who lacked the strength to get back on their feet were bayoneted or shot. Marching through the intense heat of the day drove some men so 'thirst-crazed' they broke from the column to drink the foul, scum-covered water from ponds and ditches. For this they had their brains battered out with rifle butts. Kenneth Davis, of the US State Department, describing some of the horrific scenes, told how at one terrible part of the march, men towards the rear of the column 'saw scores of headless corpses scattered along miles of road, victims of Japanese swords'.[3] Though men had nothing to eat or drink they still had to attend to the calls of nature. But at what peril! Those who halted by the wayside to relieve themselves (about half of the troops suffered from dysentery) were ordered by the guards to eat their excrement. 'They were killed if they refused to do so,' wrote Davis.

Captain William Dyess, a US fighter pilot turned infantry-man in Bataan, recalled how, as they struggled up hills gasping for breath, they were often pushed off the road into the dry ditch where they waited in the baking sun until Japanese trucks churned past, covering them with dust which caked on their sweat.[4] At the end of the first day they had covered only nine miles and had just lain down to sleep when they were shouted at, kicked and prodded with bayonets back on to the road again to march through the rest of the night.

Each day it was the same 'stop go' routine on roads congested with military traffic and for those who dropped out there was the 'clean up squad' bringing up the rear, performing their grim work of shooting those too weak to walk further.[5]

That gruesome march took a route through the hills where Claire was in hiding and so it happened that one day her friend, Pacio, came running to her and gasped out his news: 'An Igorette guide has just come over from Mariveles. He says the Japs are marching all the captured American soldiers this way!'[6] He told her that the column would probably be passing the following day and they would be able to see them with field glasses from their look-out which they manned to warn them of any Japanese patrols searching for refugees and deserters.

There was no sleep for Claire that night and at dawn she climbed up the steep rocky gradient to the look-out, hoping that she might be able to see her husband John. By the time she reached the topmost crags Claire was swaying on her feet, totally exhausted, her usually crisp, curly black hair lay plastered flat to her scalp with sweat, blood trickled from deep cuts and grazes to her hands, wrists and knees, and her heart was thumping so heavily she collapsed and lay inert just a few yards from the look-out itself. The two boys on watch covered her with a blanket and told her to rest whilst they kept watch for the approaching column.

It was five in the afternoon before one of the boys came scrambling over the rocks shouting: 'Senora! I think they're coming!' Helped by the boys, Claire climbed the last few yards up to the rough circle of rocks where over the centuries eagles had nested. She took the powerful field glasses and focused them on the dark mass filling the road in the distance below. Gradually figures took a more positive shape as they drew nearer. Claire never forgot the pictures that came into focus:

> I could now discern tall figures in the straggling middle lines, with smaller ones running along on both sides of them. Every now and then a little man would strike a tall one with the butt of his rifle, or kick him. Some of the tall men seemed to be holding up their comrades, and I saw a score of men stagger by, carrying their mates in obviously improvised litters. Occasionally a man would drop and then one of his tormentors would run a bayonet through him and kick his body from the road.

Her heart ached for the men below. Amongst them was her husband, the man she loved, had married and yet never had the comfort of holding in bed. The pain and horror of it all caused her to sink down on the rocks, sobbing. The distant crack of rifle shots brought her quickly to her feet. She snatched the binoculars, dashed the tears from her eyes and tried to make out what was happening below on the road. The picture was all too painful for her to gaze at for long. 'I saw a milling mass of men bunching together and ducking their heads to escape the blows rained on them by the butts of Jap-wielded rifles. Unable to control my emotions I handed the glasses to Pacio and sobbed, "Try to tell me what it is all about."'

She heard that the Americanos were trying to get to a water-hole at the side of the road but the Japs would not let them. Claire, with that strange feeling of wanting to look yet not wanting to look, took the glasses again. 'As I looked through them I saw an American spring from the road into the bush. Several shots were fired at him, but I did not see any signs of pursuit.' She could not stand any more. Was her husband amongst these unfortunates? Almost certainly he would be. She lay there on the ground thinking, what can I do? What can I do? Suppose some of those soldiers lying below were not dead. Suppose John …?

Weakened though she was by the previous day's climb and an earlier attack of malaria as well as from a lack of food up on the mountain, she asked two of the boys to help her down to the road to see if there were any wounded left by the Japs to die. 'We discovered the first body sprawled in an ungainly posture near the road. I looked for a dog tag or other means of identification, but there was none.' They buried that unknown soldier near a big tree, said a short prayer and then moved towards the water-hole. 'There we found three Americans dead, all without identification.' By this time Claire was too weak to go any further. Her exertions had brought on a relapse of the malaria which had afflicted nearly everyone in the mountain retreat.

The effects of her Spartan existence in the mountain were now beginning to tell; her health was seriously undermined. Scratches festered and soon became ulcers, she had been bitten by leeches and insects and at night she often lay shivering in wet clothes and in fear of the big mountain pack rats which ran over them in search of food. 'Their shrill squeaks close to our ears made chills run up and down my spine,' said Claire.

Fortunately for Claire she had that essential quality of a survivor that enabled her to think calmly and assess the facts for what they were. She realized firstly that her husband would probably be amongst that group of prisoners and secondly that by staying in the mountains she would become progressively weaker and therefore less able to be of any possible help to him and that in any case she would eventually be forced by hunger to go down into the city to seek food. Then, in a half-starved condition, she would be less able to cope. Horrified by what she had seen, she was determined to do all she possibly could to get help to her husband and to hit back hard at those hateful, loathsome Japs.

She came to a decision. The white American woman would have to disappear altogether and be replaced by someone more acceptable to the Japanese.

Once she had come to that decision she planned methodically every step she would take. Once a day she walked away from the hill-top retreat to find a secluded clearing where she could strip off all her clothing and lie in the sun. Progressively, each day, she increased the exposure time so that eventually the purposeful sun-tanning had made her as dark-skinned all over as many Filipinos.

During this transformation period she was walking through a field of high sugar cane when she came across a strange figure. An emaciated soldier with friendly twinkling eyes and a neat Vandyke beard, materialized from behind a tree trunk. For a moment she gazed at him, speechless. But it was the soldier who spoke first: 'Say, are you perhaps an American woman?'

The soldier introduced himself as John Boone of 31st Infantry. Claire's heart raced. The same regiment as her husband. Did he know John Phillips? No, sorry, he did not. They talked for some time and Claire heard how John Boone was one of the many American soldiers who had, for months, been evading the Japs. He believed that soon MacArthur would mount an offensive and they would all be able to rejoin a fighting regiment. That evening she walked back to her hill camp with a lighter heart.

A week later she was wakened in the night by a soldier who told her he had a message for her from John Boone. She was to go with him right away to his camp.

Boone had a plan which he expounded enthusiastically to Claire as soon as she arrived. He had been all over the hills and come across hundreds of American and Filipino soldiers, who were lost and starving but still had a burning desire to fight Japs. He believed he could gather them together into an effective guerilla band. What prevented him from doing this was the lack of supplies. If he had a good contact in Manila to smuggle food, clothes and medicine up to him then he could hit back hard at the Japs. They had plenty of weapons taken from the dead of both sides.

Then Boone sprang the bombshell. 'That contact in Manila could be *you*!' Claire gasped but the idea took root in her mind immediately and she began asking questions. Boone had thought everything through carefully. Claire could see that his plan would work, given the right help. And that help she was ready, eager in fact, to give.

She was all the more convinced that she made the right decision a few days later when she had another visitor at the hill camp. A priest, Father Cabagnis, who had talked to her on previous occasions when he had called to see his flock on the hill and knew of her worries over the fate of her husband, came and sat down beside her.

He was a lean, wiry man, outwardly dour but with a puckish sense of humour and Claire liked him. Though a Filipino, he talked with a Brooklyn accent. After the first few words of greeting were over he began to look more serious, saying: 'My daughter, there is something you should know.' Claire turned anxiously to face him and asked, 'Bad news, Father?'

The priest smiled, sadly perhaps but maybe a little reassuringly, before he answered, 'Not too bad ... not too good ... your husband is now a prisoner of the Japanese in Manila. At least he is alive.' He told her everything he knew about John, and that of the 70,000 who started the march northwards only 54,000 had arrived at the final camp at Cabanatuan in Manila. 'I shall keep in touch and let you know how he is from time to time.'

That clinched it. Any doubts that Claire might have had about John Boone's plan now vanished. She would go down into Manila and the sooner the better. There she could help both her husband and John Boone's guerillas.

Her journey down to the Philippine capital was accomplished with the help of Filipino traders who hid her in the bottom of their tiny sailing craft under banana leaves over which was piled the fruit they were taking down to the market. To say it was a most uncomfortable journey would be trite; it was steaming hot, insects crawled over her but she did not dare disturb the fruit in case a Japanese patrol happened to draw alongside at that moment. One did stop them in the bay of Manila. He asked questions, helped himself to fruit and then, apparently satisfied, made off. At last, after hours cramped in the bottom of the boat, Claire crawled out a sorry sight, stained with fruit juice of many colours and with ugly lumps on her arms and face where insects had bitten her. In this ragged, tramp-like state she made her way to the house of Judge Mamerto Roxas.

There, his family, once they had recognized her, took her in and made her feel most welcome. They were so hospitable that it seemed wonderful to Claire to be just alive and living a normal life where there was running water, a clean bed to sleep in and nourishing meals. Furthermore, the judge arranged for his doctor to give her a course of quinine injections and took care of all her medical expenses. His wife gave her wholesome food and soon she was feeling as fit as she ever had been. Her hosts enjoyed her company and took her in completely as one of the family. The only stipulation they made was that she should not leave the house on any pretext whatsoever. So far they had had no trouble with the Japanese and like many people in other countries occupied by enemy troops, they adopted the policy of keeping clear of confrontation. Naturally they did not want to face the dire consequences of being caught harbouring an American who should have been handed over to the commandant of the Santo Tomas internment camp.

During this period of recovery Claire had the great joy of being reunited with her daughter, Dian, and it would have been a pleasant existence to sit out the rest of the war in the comfort of that family house. The temptation was there but defying it was a far greater feeling, the memory of those prisoners on the march and the urge to help her husband now incarcerated with them. With her strength restored she felt certain that her skin was darkly tanned enough for her to pass for Spanish or Italian.

There were few Italians in Manila and although she could not speak the language she thought that there would be little chance of her being discovered for the Japanese could not speak it either.

She decided to become an Italian and telephoned a friend who worked in the Italian Consulate to ask if he could make out Italian papers so that she could pass as a national of one of Japan's allies.

A week later, Claire became 'Dorothy Fuentes', a young woman born in the Philippines of Neapolitan parents and she left the house of Judge Roxas to take up residence with her daughter in a small apartment. Her plans were well laid; she was to work as a singer – her former profession – in Ana Fey's Night Club. There she could raise money to buy food and medicine which could be smuggled into the Cabanatuan prison camp and so help her husband.

This, she soon found, was not going to be as difficult as she had imagined. The Filipinos had seen there was little point in resisting the inevitable; the philosophy generally was that the best way of surviving was to co-operate with the invader and wait patiently for things to get better. Consequently civilians were now taking jobs with the Japanese military as a semblance of normality returned to the city. Many Filipinos found work of a menial nature in Cabanatuan prison camp. Thus they were able to pass in and out quite freely every day. Soon they were smuggling medicine and food in to their friends and to others who paid them handsomely for the service. Japanese guards on the camp gates varied in their reactions to all this smuggling; some dealt harshly with any woman they discovered; others profited from bribes in the form of money or in 'home comforts' from the women when they were off duty.

Conditions in the camp were appalling; sanitation was of the crudest form with stinking open drains. The prisoners had little resistance to dysentery organisms carried by giant blue-bottles which at meal times swarmed from the open latrines to the dollops of rice in the prisoners' mess tins. Bartlett Kerr, whose father died in one of those camps, wrote of 'naked, dying men who wallowed in their own bloody excrement. Medical corpsmen had to minister to them without urinals, bed pans, toilet paper, mops or buckets.'[7]

Revolting though these details may be for the reader today, one can imagine how sickening they were for Claire Phillips who heard all about the horrific conditions, and more, from Filipinos working in the camp. It was at this time that Claire had a stroke of luck. She met Margaret Utinsky, a short bustling woman in her late thirties who would, in peace time, have been a natural candidate for president of the local Women's Institute. She too had escaped internment in the Santo Tomas camp and was also the wife of an American soldier. Her soldier husband had died in the camp at Cabanatuan but Margaret had organized a team who could smuggle food into the camp. Amongst these secret helpers was a German priest, called Father Buttenbruck, who had a permanent pass from the Japanese permitting him to enter the camp to carry out charitable work. Margaret thought he could probably get a message from Claire to her husband,

John Phillips.

Claire was now very excited at the thought of being in touch again with her husband and being able to get the right kind of food, medicine and clothing for him to recover from the ordeals of the march and starvation diet in the camp. Now she could think of nothing else. It was hard for her to believe that there had been a time when she did not know John Phillips, a time when she had wandered through the Manila streets without giving a thought to having a man in her life. In their short time together they had been supremely happy. She recalled how she had always felt a lifting of the heart when he came through the door of her house or the club where she sang. Those happy days, she mused, might one day come again.

She was standing dreamily looking over the piles of fresh fruit on a market stall one morning when her musing was interrupted by a man jostling her. He murmured excuses, and then deliberately nudged her again. Claire looked up, irritated at the rudeness. Then her eyes widened. It was a priest. He tapped her arm, half closed one eye, and motioned with his head for her to follow him.

It was Father Buttenbruck and he had a message for Claire. 'I'll be going into the camp next week. Get together a few articles that you think your husband will find useful and place them in a small shopping basket. Put a message in the bottom – not your name – but something that your husband will recognize as coming from you. Bring it to me as soon as you can.' He told her where to go.

Hastily, Claire made up a basketful of provisions: shoes, pants, socks, a shirt, toothbrush and paste, quinine, aspirin, and a few cans of food. All the way home she cudgelled her memory for a word or phrase that John would immediately recognize as from her. Then inspiration came like a flash of lightning. She wrote a short note and ended it with the words, 'I don't want to set the world on fire.' The line from the love song that had first brought them together would now reunite them.

Her spirits soared as she delivered her basket that evening to Father Buttenbruck. And as she walked homewards she felt happier than she had done for months. The heat of the day had diminished, the sun shafted brightly through gaps between the houses and she found herself humming that song again ... 'In my heart I have but one desire ... I just want to start a flame in your heart ...'. She had almost reached her apartment when she saw her daughter Dian and her amah nanny coming towards her. They ran to meet each other and hugged just alongside a Japanese truck. The driver, obviously a family man himself, smiled and spoke a few words to the amah. Claire then saw an American soldier sitting in the back of the truck with the rest of a working party. She was able to snatch a few words of conversation with him.

'Do you know Sergeant John Phillips?' she asked.

'Are you Mrs Phillips?' he asked.

Claire nodded. The soldier hurriedly continued: 'I heard about you from Margaret Utinsky. I'm Joe Rizzo, sergeant from your husband's outfit. I'm sorry. John's dead. It's true,' he whispered bluntly. 'Take it easy.' There was no time for breaking the news gently.

Claire, so buoyant a few minutes ago, stumbled away to her apartment, her eyes blurred with tears. There in the privacy of her small bedroom, a resurgence of grief came over her. Earlier, she had held back the tears, now she let them come. Gradually her anguish turned to anger, a fortifying, bitter hate. She shed tears of farewell and acceptance, of memory and love, gentle and cleansing tears which began a healing process. And then she shed tears of rage. She was not going to be beaten.

Though she could no longer help her husband, she could still help the other half-starved wretches languishing in the stinking prison camp. But that was not enough to satisfy that deep instinct within her to strike back at the men who had killed her young, dearly loved husband. She would find a way.

At night she lay awake in her bed; she had no rest, no peace of mind, obstinately determined to find a way. She even dreamt of her vengeance. But how was she to carry it out? She would not put it off.

Meanwhile though, she had to eat, earn money and look after her daughter and therefore she did not let the yearning for revenge for her lost love interfere with her work at Ana Fey's Night Club. She threw herself more energetically into her songs to escape from the pain of her grief. 'I prodded myself into a show of vivacity that stood me in good stead,' she recalled.[8] 'And it gave me a thrill to be so easily accepted in my new role as I made the rounds of the tables between my singing numbers.'

On one evening she was invited to join four Japanese civilians seated at a table. She had barely got seated when one of them told her to get some ice. Claire turned to call a waiter

Sister Vivian Bullwinkel, the only woman to survive the Banka Island massacre. She arrived back home in Australia in 1945

Brigadier Dame Margot Turner, DBE, RRC, QHNS, Matron in Chief and Director Army Nursing Service, 1964–8, accompanies Princess Margaret, Colonel in Chief, QARANC, at the opening of the Training Centre at Aldershot in October 1967

Brigadier Margot Turner receives from the Chief of the US Army Nursing Corps a plaque in recognition of her distinguished service to military nursing, Washington, 1965

Suda Bay, Crete, where the hospital stood in 'No-man's Land'
during the German assault

The caves on the sea shore between Canea and Maleme into
which the badly wounded were moved during the German air
bombardment and ground attacks. Joanna, then the only woman
nurse on Crete, continued to tend the wounded and assist at
operations

Joanna Stavridi in Spanish Infanta costume for a charity ball at the Austrian Embassy, before the war

Joanna Stavridi in her Greek Red Cross uniform

The scene near Maleme airfield, close to the hospital, at the height of the German parachute attack on Crete. The clusters of parachutes are carrying heavy equipment such as guns and vehicles. The German victory was dearly won. So heavy were the losses in men and machines that Hitler never again permitted large-scale airborne operations to be carried out

US soldiers and sailors surrender to the Japanese forces at Corregidor Island. Claire's husband was among these prisoners. (Captured Japanese picture)

American soldiers as they started out on the infamous 'March of Death' from Bataan. Some three thousand men began the march without food or water. Few finished. Claire Phillips' husband John died shortly after finishing the march. The picture was captured from the Japanese

Mrs Claire Phillips, alias 'High Pockets', who took direct action against the Japanese after her husband was taken prisoner and died in Cabanatuan prison. She was determined to repay her enemies in any way she could as a spy and a courier

American prisoners of war cheering on their liberation at Cabanatuan prison camp, January 1945

'All's well that ends well'. In November 1990, the much-loved and respected Queen Mother returned to Coventry to attend the international service of remembrance and reconciliation in the cathedral on the fiftieth anniversary of the 1940 blitz on Coventry

King George and Queen Elizabeth pick their
way among the debris caused by bombs falling
on Buckingham Palace whilst they were in
residence in September 1940

Scenes such as this typified the
welcome people gave to their King
and Queen under front-line
conditions. They could still raise a
smile and a cheer despite their ordeal
of death from the skies

'Ministers of Morale' was how the *New York
Herald Tribune* described the King and Queen at
the height of the blitz. Never were royalty closer
to their people than in the midst of the blitz. The
Queen in those terrifying months must have
talked to literally thousands of people who had
lost loved ones and homes

Special Operations Executive agent Pearl Witherington, later Mme Cornioley. At one time the Germans put a price of one million francs on her head. No one ever claimed it

Some landed by parachute but not all agents found a friendly reception committee waiting for them. All too frequently, Germans would be waiting

Violette Szabo, nee Bushell, the half-French daughter of a Brixton motorcar dealer, who was reputed to be the best shot in SOE and an outstanding character, as her posthumous George Cross testifies. She, like Pearl Witherington, was more than a courier and radio operator: she was a fighter in actual warfare

The agent pick-up plane. A Mark III Westland Lysander modified to carry agents into occupied France and pick them up at a later date

but the Japanese shouted, 'No, you,' and emphasized this demand by a hefty smack on her bottom. Furiously Claire pivoted back in her chair to face the fat, slit-eyed civilian but before she could voice her protest he pushed his glowing cigarette end on to her stockingless leg snarling, 'In Japan, women wait on men.' Unable to control herself, Claire retaliated as an American woman. 'I slapped him hard on the side of his scowling monkey face.'

That did it. It was a crowning insult for a Japanese man to be struck by a mere woman. He frothed and fumed and went across to complain to Madam Fey. Punishment would have to be administered. Now. Knowing the form and knowing that money was of more importance to her than saving the hide of one of her employees who had been stupid enough to ask for trouble, Madam Fey pointed towards the door of a room at the far end of the dance floor and told Claire to go with the men to apologize for her behaviour.

Claire reluctantly accompanied the men. She was told to sit down and for half an hour listened to a lecture in broken English that would have been comical if it had not been so ominous, for throughout the talk there were references to punishment for not learning how to act as a Japanese woman in Japanese-held territory – 'to be humble and as a servant'. When the lecture was over she was told to stand with her hands behind her. She closed her eyes as a rain of stinging blows hammered on her face and body until she slumped to the floor only partly conscious.

That chastisement taught Claire another lesson. She knew now that she could not rely upon Ana Fey for any protection whatsoever. Indeed, she heard afterwards that Ana had instructed the orchestra to play fortissimo to drown any cries that might come from the 'lecture' being delivered at the other end of the dance floor.

Once again that night, Claire lay awake seething with anger and seeking ways of getting her revenge. It was when she looked at her bruised and tear-stained face in the mirror the next morning that the idea came to her: she would be better off running her own club than working for Ana Fey. From that moment on further exciting thoughts tumbled over one another; ideas that would also satisfy her lust for teaching the Japanese a lesson or two in behaviour.

Already, in the short time that she had worked in the night club, she had noticed that Japanese officers were little different from officers in other armies – once they were off duty and had drunk a few glasses of wine, they talked more freely. If she opened a more exclusive club than Ana Fey's she would automatically attract higher ranking officers, men with information that would be of great value to John Boone's guerillas and also to General MacArthur.

Within a few days Claire Phillips was ready with plans to fight back against her enemies, not as a guerilla but *as a spy*. She had considered thoroughly the risks that would be involved and what her fate might be if she were discovered; she was also well aware of the efficient way in which the Japanese army policed its occupied areas and how highly organized were its services of counter-espionage. But her mind was made up. She would accept the risks. Thoughts of them set her heart pounding but with the excitement of it all her mind seemed to be keyed up to a keener pitch. She knew that she would have to change her whole character; to become when necessary a liar, a cheat, a thief and maybe even a murderer. All this she accepted.

There remained only the practical side of things to arrange: a place, money, and staff. Help came most unexpectedly. Chan, the owner of a Chinese restaurant that she and John used to frequent, came into the club one night and stayed behind when the doors finally closed. Claire told him of her burning desire to open her own place. She told him that her main objective was to raise funds for Boone's guerillas and to alleviate the sufferings of all those prisoners rotting in Cabantuan camp. Of spying she made no mention.

The Chinaman listened attentively to her plans and when she had finished he agreed to lend her enough money to rent a big studio room, formerly used as a dancing school and located in a fashionable part of the city near the waterfront. Two of Claire's colleagues at Ana Fey's were overjoyed when they heard of Claire's new premises and immediately offered to work for her. The news spread like wild fire. Soon workmen transformed the one-time dance school into a luxurious lounge with low-slung settees and small booths to one side for those who wanted to have a little more privacy. Fely, her loyal helper and friend from Ana Fey's, got together an orchestra and a floor show far superior to anything previously seen in Manila. Chan was generous with his loan and in a surprisingly short time the Tsubaki Club was ready for its formal opening. Claire Phillips too, the modern-day Mata Hari, was ready to go into action.

* * *

In that spring of 1942, Claire Phillips was about to discover what the intelligence agencies of all the great powers had found throughout the history of warfare, that the best information on military matters does not always come from the military intelligence pundits working behind enemy lines. Often the most precious pieces of information come from the careless lips of highly placed officers whispering sweet nothings and seductive promises into receptive ears.

Indeed, about the same time that the enthusiastic amateur spy, Claire Phillips (now better known in Manila as 'Madam Dot', the night club artiste, and to her guerilla friend Boone by her code name of 'High Pockets'), was setting up her organization for gathering information, the highly trained professional, Reinhard Heydrich, head of Germany's secret security service – the Sicherheitsdienst or SDD – was setting up his own 'Madam Kitty' in a Berlin brothel for precisely the same purpose, as he explained to his henchman SS Obersturmführer Walter Schellenberg.

> Pretty girls and hard liquor are great aids to relaxation, my friend. It takes a congenial atmosphere to thaw a man out and loosen his tongue. The younger and prettier the girl he's with, and the more he hopes to get out of her, the readier he is to unload. If we employ girls we can trust, I think we'll get a better insight into matters. I expect such an establishment to yield material of vital importance to our intelligence service.[9]

Claire Phillips had girls she could trust. She warned them to beware of neighbours and even some of their friends who were not above being seduced and enlisted by Japanese officers trading favours – such as special treatment of prisoners related to the women – for information. Claire was sure about her team. They went into action immediately the 'exclusive' Tsubaki Club opened.

It was full of senior Japanese officers from the first night onwards for, in contrast to the British army's attitude to sex and its refusal to ensure that the sexual needs of soldiers were catered for in clean, supervised brothels, the Japanese did attempt to take care of their men's sexual comforts. Drinking, organized sexual pleasure and roughneck carousing were part and parcel of the Japanese male image and consequently

Japanese authorities looked benignly upon the well-run institutions looking after their soldiers' interests. Furthermore, wherever possible they set up their own brothels, staffed with girls recruited in Tokyo's whore-houses or from local resources. Where brothels were not organized then places of relaxation, like Claire's Tsubaki Club, were treated well and rarely troubled by the police. Consequently, Claire's information-gathering went on without suspicions being aroused.

She explained:

> We operated in a methodical manner. After our hostesses had
> coaxed our high-ranking official guests into a jovial mood, either
> Fely or I would join the party and cajole the alcohol-befuddled
> Nips into talking. If they were army men, we led them on to tell
> about troop movements, and the conditions of roads and
> bridges. If naval officers, we lured them into talking about their
> ships. We pumped many newly arrived businessmen about the
> locations and nature of their establishments.[10]

Everything was just too easy. Perhaps too easy for their own safety. Whenever a new face appeared at the club then Claire would pounce with a prodigal flow of intoxicants, be delightfully friendly and flattering until eventually she would be listening to an unguarded stream of military information, rumour and gossip. She would worm out from her clients their unit and next destination. Typical of this technique, Claire later revealed, was the case of the lonesome captain.

He was a good-looking man and young for his rank but seemingly without any friends at all, for he came to the club night after night on his own. Curiosity at last overcame her; she just could not understand why this young officer should be so much on his own. One night she popped the question: 'Don't you know anyone in Manila?' Then the explanation was revealed. He had no friends whatsoever because he had just joined the regiment straight from Tokyo and knew no one in it yet. They were not too friendly to newcomers.

'That's too bad,' said Claire. 'But I can introduce you to plenty of people. Maybe you'll be stationed near enough to Manila so that you can visit here often.'

The young fish rose innocently to the bait. 'No can do,' he replied. 'Manila too far away for visit. Am going to Ringayen Gulf with regiment.'

Claire expressed surprise. 'Why should the army send you all the way up there to such a quiet place?'

Condescendingly the lonesome captain explained that women would not understand such matters but American troops might try to land there and they wanted to fortify it first.

Now Claire thought she was on to something worthwhile. She tried a little more flattery. 'But you are such a very young officer to be in charge of such an important post. With your looks you will be breaking some women's hearts.'

At this the young captain became embarrassed and modest. 'No. I only take 5,000 soldiers there. Already 30,000 stationed there. My men relieve those who are leaving.'

That was enough. The news was immediately sent to MacArthur's headquarters via Boone's guerilla radio transmitter. So pleased with this was MacArthur's intelligence chief that he began to send special instructions to Claire. She was asked, for example, to look out for a damaged Japanese aircraft carrier that might come limping into Manila's dockyard for repair. He would like to know how long the repairs would take, the destination of the carrier and its date of departure.

Here was a job for Claire's select team of amateur spies to get their teeth into. Sure enough, one evening the shy captain of the aircraft carrier came into the Tsubaki Club. He was made so welcome by Claire's friendliness, warmed by wine and made to feel so important that he responded in a most surprising manner in a very short time. He declared his love for Claire, brought her expensive presents and when Claire said they were far too good for her he replied that he could afford them for, after all, he was a highly paid captain of a big aircraft carrier and soon he would no longer be able to enjoy the company of such a beautiful and intelligent representative of one of Japan's allies. At this, Claire expressed appropriate dismay. Her sorrow at the captain's early departure showed in her face and in her halting words. She asked if the captain would let her lay on a farewell party for him and his officers the next evening.

The party went wonderfully well; the large room was crowded with laughing officers and hostesses offering a generous welcome and lavish entertainment. Claire herself joined in for she had, in a strange way, become fond of the courteous Japanese captain who talked of his family and home in Japan. She cried real tears when he left at midnight but it did not prevent her from despatching the vital intelligence immediately.

'As he and his staff departed by the front door, my runner left by the back to Boone with a note stating that the carrier was leaving at six in the morning, for Singapore and then Rabaul.'

Not all Claire's conquests were as quickly achieved or as simply. The commander of the Japanese submarine flotilla was a much harder nut to crack. He drank sparingly and talked little, and could not be beguiled into talking about his service life. Claire, with her developing experience however, felt sure that like most men who frequented night clubs, there would be one weak spot in his armour, something he kept secret but that turned him on sexually.

Casually she talked to him about other officers who came to the club and the different delights they liked to indulge in whilst away from their units, with confidence that no one would ever know of their quirkish whims. She briefly touched upon fetishes of high heels, boots, whips, massage and a variety of practices men resorted to for sexual satisfaction. But all with no apparent response from the flotilla commander.

She had all but given up when one night he came in with his slit-eyes shining excitedly, as if he had made up his mind to confide in Claire. When they were seated close together on the low-slung settee, he put his mouth close to her ear and said, 'I think I like to know you better. You singing very nice. Can you dance as well as you sing?'

Puzzled, Claire replied, 'You must be the judge of that. I am disappointed that you leave so soon. Not immediately I hope?'

The flotilla commander, his mind now firmly fixed on some sexual delight he was about to propose, unthinkingly replied, 'Tomorrow afternoon if repairs finished. There is one thing though can make me stay day longer. Can you do fan dance? If you do fan dance I bring all my officers for party tomorrow night. Tell Admiral repairs not finished.'

Claire, who had never seen a fan in her life, agreed. 'How many places shall I reserve for you and your officers, commander?' The answer surprised Claire.

'Forty.'

Forty officers meant a really big flotilla of submarines. And before many minutes had passed a runner was leaving by the back door, taking the news to Boone's guerillas in the hills. Claire though had other problems to solve. Where on earth was she going to get fans for herself and other dancers to use before the next evening? And how were they going to learn what to do with them? She called her secret team together. This was important. Somehow they had to put on a good show and keep the officers riveted to their seats until the next morning. Fely came to the rescue. She had seen fan dancers at Ana Fey's club. Two girls were sent to find split bamboo canes, others were set to work binding them together in the shape of a fan and another girl dressed the frames with pink American toilet paper which someone had filched before the Japanese invasion. Dawn had broken before they all went to bed.

They were up early the next day for a few quick rehearsals, under Fely's tutoring. All they needed to decide then was whether to be completely nude or whether under low lighting they could get away with a flesh-coloured body stocking. And for the Japanese they decided that was enough.

When the officers arrived, however, it looked as though all their preparations had been in vain. The commander immediately announced they could stay for only a short time for they had orders to sail right away. Claire realized that all her intelligence-gathering about the flotilla would be useless if headquarters were denied adequate time to act effectively in response.

The hour of sailing would have to be delayed. Claire briefed her team again. Drinks were spiked, officers tempted into a side room for special favours, the fan dance went into encores with fans 'accidentally' dropped amid much confusion; even the clock on the wall reminding them of the time was knocked off its nail and broken on the floor. It was not long before Japanese naval officers were keeling over on the low-slung settees and it was a very sleepy commander indeed who finally led his officers away from the fan dance party at six o'clock the following morning.

For days Claire wondered what had happened to them all. Certainly the flotilla had somehow sailed. It was more than a month later that Claire heard what was the outcome of that party and their delaying tactics. A submarine commander came into the Tsubaki Club and gloomily related the story. He had been on that ill-fated voyage. Every submarine in the flotilla had been lost with their crews. He was one of the few lucky ones, having been picked up by a Japanese fishing boat.

Now Claire felt she was really hitting back hard at the men who had killed her husband. Furthermore, in doing so, she had found a most satisfying feeling of engaging in high adventure, in pitting her wits against the most expert makers of war. She, a mere wife and night-club singer, now had to be counted as surely as though she were a flotilla commander herself. Every night her team of trusty hostesses was learning about the movement of military units, casualties, morale, and supplies. And at the end of each evening, reports went to guerilla headquarters.

Meanwhile, however, the Japanese counter-espionage service had been hard at work. Prompted by rebukes about formidable leaks of information in his district, the senior Japanese intelligence officer was taking desperate measures to stop the leakage. He gave orders for police and counter-espionage agents to exercise greater severity in the scrutiny and searching of suspects. People were arrested at random, searched and threatened.

Claire heard of Filipinos she knew who had been arrested and shot. The effect on her, naturally, was depressing but it did not deter her from her cause. And at a time when it might have been more prudent of her to play a quiet, waiting game she continued to expose herself to greater risks. She instituted a new service for immediate delivery of urgent military information and enlarged her espionage group.

The strain, though, was beginning to tell upon her nerves. 'I knew that my luck had been stretched like a rubber band and I did not know at what moment it would snap.' She had not long to wait. The rubber band snapped one day when one of her messengers, Helen Petroff, a Russian married to an American sailor, was arrested and taken to Fort Santiago. In her pocket was incriminating evidence. One of Claire's group, Dr Atienza, rushed over to the Tsubaki Club to warn her. 'You're sure to be the next to be arrested and we don't want that to happen. We say you must go to the hills with Dian, and let the guerillas hide you.'

The temptation was great. Claire had already done enough for her country to be grateful. Her efforts had been recorded and praised. Now she could have retired with honour, but just as Joanna Stavridi refused to sail away from Crete at the height of the battle and Diana Rowden decided against seeking sanctuary in Switzerland when she was so near the border as Gestapo teams were rounding up her Resistance group, so Claire Phillips elected to stay and not run away. Later she explained why. 'I felt that I owed it to the memory of my departed husband to remain and help his former comrades regardless of any serious consequences to myself.'

But from that moment on she knew the real meaning of fear.

On 23 May 1944, she was coaxing her child to eat a little more of her breakfast when she stopped with the spoon poised midway between Dian's basin and her mouth, not certain why, except for a sudden chilling instinct that something was wrong, something out of place, an unaccustomed sound. Morning sunshine shafted brightly through the slatted blinds, the street outside was quiet. Quiet! Too quiet. Alarm bells rang inside her head. She had seen it happen many times before – a whole block cordoned off by the police making a raid. An urgent frantic shout cut across the uncanny silence. A mother calling her child who had run out on to the street. Another shout this time. A harsh, high-pitched voice of a Japanese soldier.

'Oh Jesus!' Claire breathed. Now she knew.

Suddenly there was a clattering and thumping of boots on the stairs, a loud, insistent battering on the door. Breathless, tense, Claire went towards it. Dian, her little face screwed up in fear, watched. Claire turned the door handle. In what seemed a single moment the room was full of soldiers, Kempei Military Police. Two of them sprang towards her, poking their pistols in her ribs. '*Jittao shita ori!*' – 'Don't move!' – they shouted.

Instinctively, Claire raised her arms high, her hands facing forwards. An officer ran his hands swiftly over her dress, front and back, outside and inside her legs, searching for concealed weapons.

'You are Madame Tsubaki?' he asked. Claire nodded. 'Then come with us.'

'But my child …?' Claire began. 'Can I call my girl to look after her?'

'Hai! But no try to get away. I no mind shooting woman.'

Guards followed Claire into her maid Flora's room. Claire told her she was being arrested and that she was to look after Dian, and then swiftly and staring meaningfully at Flora, whispered one word: 'Boone!'

Claire was led away with barely time to turn to Dian and say, 'Be a good girl and Mummy will be home soon.' The picture of that tear-stained, frightened little face stayed vividly imprinted in Claire's mind during the terrifying months that followed.

The cell was bare and cold. In the centre of the floor was a small hole through which a small trickle of water flowed, the sole concession to sanitation. No bed, no chair, no bedding. Claire sat with her back to the wall and waited. Hours went by. She was hungry, cold and thirsty. Her morning coffee had not been tasted before the police came. Now she yearned for it.

Suddenly there was a shout from a guard down the corridor. Footsteps followed. The cell door creaked open and a wizened guard came in and tied a blindfold over her eyes. Claire then had visions of the cold steel of the executioner's sword, with its broad and slightly curved blade. She was pushed forward, face against the wall. More footsteps echoed and came into the room. There was the clanking sound of metallic objects against the flagstoned floor. A block? Instruments of torture? Claire's mind raced over possibilities. Her dry lips moved in prayer.

Suddenly a sharp voice came from her right-hand side, in English. 'Sit down. The chair's behind you.'

Another voice, in English, then said: 'We know all about you, "High Pockets". Answer our questions truthfully and you will soon go home.' The voices sounded vaguely familiar and for reasons of their own it seemed they did not want her to see who it was asking the questions. Hence the blindfold. The interrogators could have been patrons of the Tsubaki, Japanese who had been educated in America.

'We know that you are not Italian. What is your right name? Why are you sometimes called Claire? Who is this person "High Pockets"? Tell us how the letters signed by "High Pockets" are sent from Tsubaki.' The questions came like strokes of a whip, one after another without time for her to reply. Desperately she tried to speak but even before she got out a few words she was grabbed and thrown roughly to the ground.

'Stand up. Now tell us …' The questions this time came more slowly and deliberately. Claire knew she must stick as close to the truth as she dared. She told them she was an American by birth but had renounced her American loyalties and embraced Philippine citizenship a year ago, which in fact she had done when changing her identity.

'I am now called Dorothy Claire Fuentes.'

'Now we are getting somewhere,' said the English-speaking voice. 'Now let us have the names of the others in your group. Speak now and we will let you off more lightly. Be stubborn and we will bring your child here and make her suffer too.' Claire prayed that by now Fely or Flora would have spirited Dian away to Boone in the hills. The rest of the group had agreed that if ever anyone was captured they would not remember any names or know of any organization gathering information. Now the moment of truth had arrived. She had known the risks. She knew what would happen if she were caught. But had she really imagined in her most fearful moments what interrogation by the Japanese Secret Service was in reality? She was about to find out.

The questioners left her as suddenly as they had arrived. Their parting words struck terror into her shuddering body. 'We shall come back and ask you the questions again. Then you will be pleased to tell us everything.'

Days passed and became weeks. Still they had not come back. The number of prisoners had doubled. They were fed on two cups of rice slop a day. Everyone became progressively thinner and weaker. Claire decided that she must do something before she wasted away completely. Her chance came when a certain Captain Kobioshi did his rounds of the cells. She recognized him as an officer who used to come to the Tsubaki. But he did not recognize her now. She called to him by name and asked that her investigation be continued.

The next day she was called to his office. He told her that if she told the truth and answered all the questions, she would be let out of prison very quickly. The first questions gave her no trouble. She answered them without incriminating anyone at all. Then came the difficult ones. 'Who is "Everlasting"?'

'I don't know him by any other name.'

Kobioshi shouted. A guard came in with a thick bamboo rod and began beating her about the head and shoulders. Other questions followed and again she was able to give simple answers. But now no one believed she was speaking the truth. The inquisitor barked an order. Two guards ran out and came back with rope and a length of hose pipe. They lashed Claire down with her back to a bench, rammed the hose pipe in her mouth and held her head. The water gushed into her mouth. Claire held her breath but a guard noticed and thumped her in the stomach. Now she had to gulp the water down, drowning on dry land until her brain seemed to be swimming and mercifully she passed out.

When she came to her senses her thighs pulsed with burning sores. Japanese resuscitation techniques involved the placing of glowing cigarette ends to the fleshy parts of her legs.

The next day she was brought back for further questioning, and it was only then that Claire realized she wasn't really being questioned about her spying but about smuggling food into the Cabanatuan prison and her contacts with the guerillas. A message to the prisoners which they had intercepted puzzled them. 'Who is this person "Cal" and the American "Demi John"?' Claire almost laughed. She tried to explain that 'cal' was short for 'calamansi', a kind of syrup made from boiling oranges which was sent to prisoners in big bottles called demi-johns, to help those suffering from scurvy.

To her amazement they did not believe her. She was kicked and beaten again, as questions were repeated: 'Who are your contacts? Who is this American Demi John? Who are your contacts with the guerillas?' Slivers of wood were then slid under her fingernails and with each denial the sensitive nerve endings in her finger tips sent burning pain sensations all over her body. She could only gasp out that she knew no more than the code names she had heard.

The torture stopped. Her inquisitor looked at his colleagues and raised his eyebrows. He nodded.

'Well, since there is nothing further you can tell us there is nothing left to do but go ahead with your execution.'

She was blindfolded, dragged down a long corridor, down many old, uneven steps into a cell which seemed to open on to the river which could be heard lapping over the flagged floor. Claire had seen for herself the mutilated bodies floating down the river Pasig. She stopped listening to the guards saying this was the last chance she would have of saving herself and started praying.

'Kneel down, bow your head. Two minutes to decide.'

A rough hand brushed her hair from the nape of her neck. She felt the cold, sharp steel of the beheading sword laid tentatively against her neck and then lifted. Her last thoughts were 'So this is it.'

Nature, at times, has a way of protecting the mind from unbearable trauma. There is so much the human brain can stand before it blacks out and at that moment the reflexive reaction saved Claire. When she recovered her senses she was back in the cold, damp cell reserved for prisoners still under interrogation before trial by court martial. There were to be no more questions. She was taken to Fort McKinley, arraigned before a Japanese court to answer the preferred charges. When asked what she had to say, she began to explain that she was only sending medicine and food to men less fortunate than herself when she was struck violently across the mouth, breaking a front tooth. 'You required to say you guilty,' admonished the president of the court.

That was that. She pleaded guilty and was sentenced to be shot as a spy. The satisfaction that the president seemed to be relishing as he burbled out her sentence was somewhat cut short, however, by an unexpected interruption from above. There was a roaring in the sky and explosions rocked the courthouse. For three hours bombs rained down, wrecking the whole area. But the explosions seemed to have disturbed something else too – changed people's minds perhaps.

Claire was taken from the courtroom to the Women's Correctional Institution, a penitentiary for time-serving prisoners and it dawned on Claire then that she was not going to be shot after all. Her sentence was read to her in her cell by the governor: 'Because of the mercy of His Imperial Highness, the Emperor of Japan, your sentence has been commuted to twelve years' hard labour …'

The retribution that was clearly speeding towards Claire's torturers had obviously given them second thoughts. Conditions in that prison were still appalling; the daily diet was rice gruel for breakfast, a small portion of rice and boiled cassava roots at noon and boiled weeds with thin rice soup for dinner.

The woman who had gone through so much for her patriotism and determination to fight back was now wasting away.

After eight months and eighteen days she weighed a mere ninety-five pounds. She lay motionless on her bed with barely enough energy to move and it was in this state one day that she heard from afar someone shouting. The noise came from across the courtyard where a voice was shouting, 'Americans. *Vivos los Americanos!*'

General MacArthur had redeemed his promise. He had come back.

American army doctors gave Claire a thorough medical examination. They found her to be anaemic, suffering from scurvy and several varieties of skin infection, in need of dental care to rebuild her broken teeth, and dangerously emaciated.

She was put on a nourishing diet and a generous supply of medication but the best kind of therapy came one day with the chaplain of Santo Tomas internment camp. He brought it to her himself in his arms – her daughter Dian.

7

Front Line Fighters

Not many women who seemed promising enough
from SOE's point of view to be worth interview
would be likely to quail at the thought of a singularly
nasty death, perhaps preceded by outrageous torture
if caught; and fighting enthusiasm can be quite as
strong in one sex as in the other.

Professor M.R.D. Foot[1]

Just like the Japanese in the Pacific, the Germans when they
occupied a country brought with them something more than
weaponry; they brought a doctrine, a regime which they
sought to impose by rule of fear. They were helped always by
self-seeking acolytes like the Milice Police in France, who could
be just as harsh with their compatriots as the Germans
themselves. Hitler's aim for each newly structured state was to
become a subordinate part of the 'Thousand Year Reich' of his
dream. Of all the leaders in modern history none had ruled
conquered people with so much savagery.

Experience proved, however, that rule by fear, instead of
daunting the human spirit, strengthened it. The flow of recruits
to Resistance groups grew in direct proportion to the severity
of reprisals against those fighters. The battle lines then were
clear; all those who collaborated with Germany were just as
much the enemy as the Germans themselves. By a vicious
circle of events greater Resistance activity brought increasingly
savage reprisals which in turn brought more recruits to the
Resistance fighters in all countries occupied.

Brutal oppression simply did not work. General Lammerd-
ing, commanding the Das Reich 2nd SS Division which
perpetrated some of the most obscene atrocities, claimed that:
'It was necessary to provoke terror among the Maquisards to
deprive them of the support of the civil population.'[2] But he

was proved wrong. His cruel 'remedial' lessons failed to teach an increasingly aggressive Resistance movement that the risks of sabotage and ambushing German troops were prohibitive. And as these fighting guerilla groups grew in size one thing became clear: they needed to be more centrally organized, as we saw in Chapter 1. They needed to have their activities co-ordinated for maximum effect, they needed experienced leaders, properly trained saboteurs and the right kind of equipment.

Today one tends to forget that these groups of guerilla fighters in France, usually called 'the Maquis', were originally just bands of young men who had fled to the mountains to avoid being sent into the German labour service. They took refuge in the forests and mountains, building log cabins, camping in deserted derelict houses and generally living rough – short of food and water. In the early days the Germans thought these small groups of men of little consequence, merely outlaws, and never considered they would one day become a menace.

Britain's SOE saw their potential however. They were just the right calibre of men to receive parachute drops of arms and ammunition and they had the manpower to whisk these quickly away into hiding places close to their mountain retreats. Consequently, soon after 1940, contacts were being made for this express purpose. The next stage was to train them to fight with those arms against enemy units so that Germany would never again feel she had complete control of her rear areas or lines of communication.

From 1941 onwards, selected personnel of Britain's SOE and later America's OSS (Office of Strategic Services) played an important role in organizing the secret armies on efficient lines. And in this role, women were in the forefront yet again. They fought with machine guns and grenades alongside their Maquis comrades against front-line German regiments.

This was one of the best kept secrets of the war. Neither the public nor British Parliament was ever aware of the hazardous work being done by women until the British Secretary of State for Air shocked the House of Commons on 6 March 1946 with an unusual revelation. To the packed benches he said:

The women's Auxiliary Air Force[3] has been to the forefront of these activities. Several young WAAF officers were dropped by parachute at night. In one case, after parachuting into France to act as a courier, a WAAF officer took charge of a large Maquis group after the capture of her commanding officer, re-organized it, and, displaying remarkable qualities of tact, leadership and courage, contributed to the success of many supply-dropping operations and to the destruction of the enemy forces.

Strange though it may seem today, the members were not very surprised to hear of the heroic exploits of those women. Dame Irene Ward, MP, was in the House that day and later wrote:

I can't recall that anyone displayed undue astonishment at hearing that women were operating in the heart of enemy territory. I think by then we had become so accustomed to women's part in the war effort that we had ceased to be surprised at any unusual job they had undertaken. The country had moved a long way from the day when Ernest Bevin had so emphatically stated to me that women's part in the war effort would be a *very limited one*.

Perhaps one reason for the lack of surprise manifested on the faces of those members seated in the warm debating chamber, so far removed from the clatter of machine guns and the smell of battle, was the difficulty of translating the cold, formal words of the Secretary of State's announcement into the bloody reality of war at the sharp end.

Some of the women who did know what it was like were Yvonne Baseden, Christine Granville, Violette Szabo, Nancy Wake and Pearl Witherington.

Pearl it was who took charge of the Maquis group of between two and three thousand strong mentioned by the Secretary of State, and she distinguished herself so well in the fighting that she was recommended for the Military Cross – a medal for which women were supposed to be ineligible. But then Pearl was a most remarkable woman.

She was the eldest of four daughters born to British parents living in Paris. In 1939 she was holding a responsible secretarial post to the air attaché in the British Embassy's Paris office. The speed of the German advance caught the Witherington family still in the city when it was occupied in June 1940. The Witheringtons, though, were not the sort of family to sit back and allow themselves to be interned. They were going to get to Britain and 'do their bit'. On 9 December 1940, as German news bulletins were reporting the Luftwaffe's devastating attacks on

London and all Britain's major ports, the Witheringtons left Paris for their long journey to Britain.

First they had to move into the unoccupied zone of France. It was not easy to cross the Demarcation Line from German-occupied France into the unoccupied zone; to go by train you needed a pass which was closely scrutinized; travellers by road found that all cars and lorries were searched. The easiest way to cross the Demarcation Line was to go by night, creeping across the fields guided by smugglers who knew where the German patrols and their dogs would be at certain times. To be caught was to risk a prison sentence.

Eventually Pearl got her family across and bought tickets to Marseilles with the last bit of their remaining money. Consequently they arrived in the south of France hungry and penniless. Pearl took the initiative, went directly to the British Consul there and came away with money and something more. She had got herself a job!

Now the family could gather themselves for the next stage of their journey. It was to be by means of a Red Cross ship to Spain, which was expected shortly. But daily they were disappointed. Pearl carried on working at the Consulate in a secretarial capacity and the family lived in a cheap Marseilles hotel of a rather dubious character. The food was often of a 'dubious' nature too, but the French have a way of making horse meat and lungs taste like something out of the Ritz. 'The lights in wine sauce were delicious,' recalled Pearl's sister, Jacqueline.[4]

The time came when they could wait no longer. The contingency plan was put into operation. They would make the gruelling trip overland through the Pyrenees to Spain and Portugal. Eventually the family arrived in Lisbon safely and from there took a trawler to Gibraltar. Fortunately for them a troopship was about to leave for Britain and room was made for the Witheringtons. They sailed into Glasgow on 14 July 1941 and two weeks later, on 1 August, Pearl's two younger sisters, Mimi and Jackie, joined the WAAF. These two young women were not allowed to slip quietly into their training, however. Someone somewhere got wind of their journey home and before long the press had gathered in force at their recruit training station at RAF Bridgnorth.

National newspapers hailed them as 'heroines' and carried their story headlined 'They walked a thousand miles to join the WAAF.' Little did they know that the one girl not mentioned in that heroine story would soon be making a much bigger name for herself.

Pearl Witherington had gone quietly to the Air Ministry and got herself a job similar to the one she had held in Paris. Eventually however she found the routine boring and looked around for a more challenging form of service. She had heard, through her contacts with the Foreign Office, vague talk about the possibility of special operational duties in France and so she went to see the Directorate of Allied Air Co-operation to ask if she could volunteer for such work. She drew a point-blank refusal. Few people then knew about the Special Operations Executive and they recruited in strange ways.

Dame Irene Ward, MP, gave a classic example of how recruits became involved:

> Mrs Peggy Smith, train wrecker and Nazi killer, the daughter of an army officer, and born in Paris, was at a party in the lounge of a London hotel; she saw one of the guests drop a book, and because it had a French title she returned it to its owner with a few French words. Her good accent was commented on and before the party broke up she was asked if she would like to ring up the officer who owned the book.[5]

As this young lady was bored with her WAAF duties, she telephoned the number given to her and met a popular novelist of that day, Selwyn Jepson, who had taken on a new job as chief 'talent spotter' for SOE. Peggy soon found herself to be the latest recruit for training as an F Section agent.

Pearl had not yet found an entry to that select band but she did not allow herself to be put off by her first rebuff. She made further discreet enquiries from a friend who worked in the Foreign Office and discovered that the answer to her problem of how to get back into France might lie inside the Marks and Spencer's building, Michael House, at 82 Baker Street. The house backed on to a scruffy, narrow side-alley with a doorway bearing a plaque of black marble indicating the presence of an obscure department going under the name of 'Inter-Services Research Bureau'. Through this doorway went men and women in civilian clothes, rarely anyone in uniform.

Pearl went in. She was fired by an inner fury against the Germans, as she later recalled:

> I was furious at the way they had behaved in France. People who never lived in a country occupied by Germans can have no idea what it was like. They took whatever they wanted.

Everything disappeared. There was no liberty. You never knew what restrictions were going to be levied from one day to the next. And there was always that fear. The knock on the door in the middle of the night after which people disappeared. It roused in me such a fury that we had to get away from Paris and do something about it. I literally pushed my way into SOE.[6]

In a small room on the top floor of Michael House she found a tall, gentle man with a self-deprecating manner, a man in his late thirties with thinning hair, who invited her to sit down and tell him what she wanted. He was Colonel Maurice Buckmaster, Head of F Section, SOE.

Maurice Buckmaster had left Eton in his early teens and taken a post as reporter with *Le Matin* in Paris after his father had been declared bankrupt. From *Le Matin* Maurice had drifted to banking and then became manager of the Ford Motor Company's headquarters in Paris. When war broke out he served with the British Expeditionary Force and came out through Dunkirk. Shortly afterwards he had had a talk with Colonel Templar, the future Chief of the Imperial General Staff at the War Office, and assumed command of F (for French) Section, SOE, in September 1941, with special responsibility for selecting agents.[7]

He let Pearl talk, interrupting rarely, and it was soon evident to him that here was a woman who was ideal for the sort of work he had in mind. He advised her to return to the Air Ministry and await a call for training.

When that call came, Pearl had to report for a probationary period at Wanborough Manor during which all potential agents were subjected to close scrutiny of their behaviour at all times of day and night. Was it really that of a French woman or man? Their reactions were carefully noted. They were offered drinks to see what effect alcohol had upon them, they were roused from sleep in the middle of the night to discover whether they cried out in French or in English. On top of all the rigorous physical and technical training there were the little points of social behaviour to revise. Marcel Ruby recalled: 'How did the would-be agent act at the dinner table, for instance? Did he, as a Frenchman would, wipe the gravy with a piece of bread and eat it with gusto, or did he, in proper English manner, leave a few chips or *petits pois* on the plate, and carefully align his knife and fork at half-past six?'[8]

It took four or five months to transform an honest citizen into a ruthless and redoubtable Resistance warrior. No one was passed out until all departments of the training team were satisfied that the trainee was competent in the specialist techniques as well as being able to pass muster as genuinely French. Pearl, with her Paris background, passed out with distinction.

During these months Pearl's family were mystified. They did not have a clue as to what was going on, nor did the neighbours, for as Pearl's sister Jackie recalled: 'Sometimes Pearl would come home dressed in the smart khaki uniform of the First Aid Nursing Yeomanry, and then at other times she was in the light blue of a commissioned officer in the WAAF. Then she just disappeared!'[9]

On 23 September 1943 Pearl was called to RAF Tempsford in Bedfordshire, a highly camouflaged airfield occupying a strip of land between the main London to Edinburgh railway line and the Great North Road. There the RAF Special Duties squadron had a four-engine Halifax waiting to take her back to France and into action.

She had completed her parachute training jump from the metal cab swaying silently beneath the balloon tethered at 800 feet, which was like plummeting straight down a lift shaft, and the less frightening ones from the aircraft where the drop is diagonally sideways. And no doubt her confidential report would read something like 'Nervous but controlled', as so many did.[10]

Now she was going to need all the control she could muster as she went through the pre-flight rituals and final briefing. The last items of her equipment were handed over and she was ready. Soon she would be on her own. Dusk had turned into night. A small Hillman personal utility truck drew up to take her to the runway where the huge Halifax bomber stood waiting.

Pearl climbed aboard. Away to the right of the airfield a green light flickered. The pilot rammed the throttle levers open, revving the engines to full power. The fuselage by Pearl's side shuddered, brakes came off and the aircraft rolled slowly forward, gathering speed with each second as it raced towards the 125 miles per hour 'unstick' speed. Then it was up, rising slowly to vanish into the darkness of night.

Soon, far below, a friendly light flashed, winking 'goodbye' from the last dark headland. She was committed.

She had been entrusted with a particularly important

assignment. Her duties were not those of radio operator or courier but as liaison officer to her commanding officer, Squadron Leader Maurice Southgate who was responsible for a vast and scattered area ranging from the Loire near Orléans to the Dordogne and with a detachment bordering the Pyrenees. Fortunately for Pearl, Maurice Southgate was no stranger to her. She had known him when she was at the Air Ministry and had learnt there of the high regard in which he was held.

Furthermore, Maurice Southgate's background was similar to her own. Born of British parents in Paris, he had grown up there and become a furniture designer by profession. On the outbreak of war he had rushed back to Britain to enlist in the British Army and crossed to France with the first batch of the British Expeditionary Force. On the evacuation he survived the sinking of the troopship *Lancastria*. Two years later, at the age of twenty-nine, he was recruited into SOE by Colonel Buckmaster and was then given an honorary commission in the Royal Air Force Volunteer Reserve.

It is now said to be part of the SOE folklore that due to the clerical delay attending this transfer from the Army to the RAF and to the fact that he himself was not quite sure to which of the two services he really belonged, he wore Army and RAF uniforms on different days (as Pearl Witherington had done too) while staying with his mother in London. A neighbour observed to Mrs Southgate one day: 'I never see your two sons go out together.'[11]

Now Southgate was exceptionally busy developing a circuit around Chateauroux in the Indre region and at the same time exploring the possibilities of a circuit based on the towns of Tarbes and Pau in the foothills of the Pyrenees. With armed Maquis groups in such a huge area to co-ordinate he really did need an efficient liaison officer to work with him. Pearl Witherington fitted the bill ideally. There was another reason, however, for his choice, a factor which Pearl was going to appreciate when she landed. But, in the shuddering confines of the Halifax that evening she had no idea what Southgate had laid on for her.

Now the Halifax was flying low in a clear, star-speckled sky. The RAF despatcher, typically a cheerful young man exuding confidence and *bonhomie*, came to check the webbing on her parachute harness, tightening a buckle here, tugging another elsewhere, carefully following the static line through his hands to its dog-lead attachment on the fixed point wire on the fuselage and finally giving her a reassuring tap on the shoulder and a serene smile conveying all was well. Next he opened the exit panel; cold air and a roaring of engines rushed in. Minutes ticked by slowly. Suddenly the red light came on: 'Action stations'. No sooner was Pearl braced ready than the command came: 'Go!'

Acting with the reflexive muscle movement ingrained by her parachute training, she was out, passing beneath the tail wheel. There was a flurry of silk and the canopy blossomed above her. 'I sighed with relief that I'd got out without breaking my nose on the other side of the exit hole – as sometimes happened to parachutists then,' she recalled.[12] Down she sailed in the chill of the night air towards the moonlit fields and hedges from which shadowy figures were running.

The first of the figures to meet her was her new chief, Maurice Southgate, who quickly released her parachute harness, gathered her canopy ready for stowing away and hurriedly drove her by car to a farmhouse in the next département.

What happened next could have been taken straight out of a wartime romantic film in which the heroine opens the door, walks into a warm kitchen and stands stock-still, stunned by the sight before her eyes. There, with a broad grin spreading from ear to ear, was the childhood sweetheart she had 'lost' nearly four years earlier when she had left Paris – Henri Cornioley.

He had later been captured by the Germans, imprisoned in a POW camp, escaped and then joined the French under-ground.[13] Vera Atkins, the WAAF squadron officer of the French Section of SOE with the designation of 'intelligence officer' which covered a multitude of duties including, it now seemed, that of Cupid, had been responsible with Southgate for arranging for their romantic reunion and for them to be working together.

They were to operate in the northerly part of Southgate's 'Stationer' territory near the town of Châteauroux. There Pearl, code-named 'Marie', was brought in right away to use her charm on a particularly difficult and irascible French colonel, nominally the local Maquis leader. His group was in need of being reorganized and re-equipping. Previous attempts to introduce changes had met with a stubborn reluctance to countenance any changes whatsoever.

Pearl had a way with such men. Very soon he was mouthing

the orders she composed! At the same time she was covering a wide area, liaising with other groups. She had only been 'in the field' a few weeks when a message came from SOE headquarters in London recalling Southgate for urgent consultations. Pearl remained in France, busier than ever, and throughout the winter months of 1943–4 she played a real soldier's role. She gave weapon training to new recruits, organized reception committees for drops of arms and ammunition, selected sabotage targets and often went out with explosives and fuses and placed the charges against railway lines and bridges herself. No front-line soldier did more.

Pearl, in Maurice Southgate's words, had always been a 'soldier'. She led and fought alongside her part-time soldiers in repeated skirmishes with and battles against regular German infantry units. By this time the demand for arms by Resistance groups was outstripping supply and SOE could not afford to drop a consignment into the hands of German troops who might have been alerted to the arrival. So a complicated 'fail safe' procedure was adopted. Briefly, it went like this: London would warn a Resistance group to listen to a coded BBC broadcast at seven o'clock in the evening and to a second broadcast at nine o'clock on one of the three nights following. The first message would tell the leader to assemble his reception committee and the second broadcast at nine o'clock would tell him which of the selected dropping zones would be used.

Listening to the BBC was prohibited on pain of severe punishment, and because BBC broadcasts were being constantly jammed by German transmitters, it was difficult. Consequently, several radio sets had to be used in the group; this meant more people taking risks but it was unavoidable if they were to be sure of receiving an accurate message of where and when the drop would be made. On those nights, agents like Pearl Witherington were put at great risk not just by listening, but by cycling about the countryside gathering a team together, and ultimately going with them to the dropping zone, all the time hoping to avoid running into a patrol of Milice or German security police.

Once the reception party had been gathered, off they went in an old van or commodious taxi, taking the precaution of being unarmed in case they were stopped and searched on the way out. As an added precaution, the van would carry spare number plates so that they could be changed if suspicion had been aroused and a chase ensued. Vehicles would be parked off the road and under trees, facing in the direction of the return trip. Then, at the appointed hour the party would go into the fields with their torches – a white one to give the pilot the code letter in morse and the others to indicate the approach and wind direction.

Then they waited.

At last they would hear the rumble of a four-engine bomber. Lights would flash and the aircraft would roar in at 500 feet, containers falling under parachutes across the field. Men would run to each and bring it back to the waiting van, now with its engine running. Finally one container would be opened and a weapon and ammunition handed to each member of the party so that they could fight their way through any road-block they might encounter.

The journey back was a series of stops at various farms, houses, barns and even churchyards to hide the arms in every kind of nook and cranny imaginable. Finally, when the van was empty they would all go back to one farmhouse – like bomber crews returning to base – and have a substantial 'breakfast' of ham, sausage, omelette and cheese, washed down with raw red wine. This was the usual routine for the drops. 'I'll never forget those feasts – rare treats in those days – especially after all our physical exertions,' wrote Marcel Ruby.[14]

What a way to unwind!

Amongst the arms and ammunition dropped to Pearl's group in the winter of 1943–4 was a completely new weapon, one which could do the work of a squadron of heavy RAF bombers – plastic explosive, the guerilla's delight. One woman, with a mere 200 grams of this miraculous new substance and a detonator in her handbag, had tremendous destructive potential at her disposal. And now that the activities of guerilla groups were being efficiently co-ordinated, devastating attacks could be made on all forms of transport – railways, trains, dockyards and tunnels. The point is made impressively by a comparison related by M.R.D. Foot:

Nineteen Lancasters, of 617 Squadron, each with a crew of seven, bombed a target marked by Group Captain Cheshire in a Mosquito with a crew of two. One of the nineteen Tallboy bombs (12,000 pounders) blew in the mouth of an important railway tunnel near Saumur, the others made impressive holes in the surrounding fields ... The same tactical result could have been achieved without risking one hundred and thirty-five of the finest bomber aircrew in the world, through the agency of the WAAF flying officer who was commanding SOE's nearby 'Wrestler' circuit. Rail cuts were a speciality of hers.[15]

Pearl had taken over command of the large guerilla group due to an unfortunate lapse in concentration and vigilance on the part of her chief, Maurice Southgate.

SOE agents had to be constantly on the alert. They could never afford to give themselves the luxury, for example, of dozing on a long train journey or even reading a book in case they were caught momentarily off guard. Suspicion of everyone and everything was the key to avoiding capture. Naturally this imposed a tremendous strain on men and women who had been in the field for a long period. Inevitably there were lapses of concentration.

Maurice Southgate made his on May Day, 1944. He hurried to Paris to see his assistant wireless operator there and before entering the house he forgot to check that the danger signal was not flying. Agents had to protect each other from being lured into a trap and it was an accepted rule that no agent was to visit another if one of these danger signals were displayed, indicating that the Milice or Gestapo were already in the house or watching it. Simple signals – a shutter opened or closed, a towel drying on a window sill – could alert a visitor and give him time to turn away and escape. On that hot May Day of 1944 Maurice Southgate, in his haste, forgot to look for the pre-arranged signal and walked straight into the house, straight into the arms of the Gestapo. He was identified, arrested and manacled hand and foot before being taken off to Gestapo Headquarters in the Avenue Foch, Paris.

Pearl, fortunately, had not accompanied her chief, nor had his principal wireless operator, Amedee Maingard, a 25-year-old Mauritian, who was ready to go but decided against it because Pearl had told him frankly that he looked worn out and needed a rest. They made the best use of the free afternoon by going for a picnic and a swim. By this lucky decision both survived at a critical time just before D-Day and the invasion of Normandy. With Southgate gone, Amedee and Pearl divided his Stationer circuit into two, 'Wrestler' for Pearl and 'Shipwright' for Amedee Maingard.

Pearl Witherington now had sole command of the whole area of the Indre at a time when the Gestapo were especially vigilant. They knew that SOE activity was increasing and believed it to be connected with the forthcoming Allied landings to which they had been alerted by their Intelligence units and also by the systematic aerial bombardment of railway junctions and vital communications. They also reasoned that guerilla activity would be more concentrated in those areas where attacks on their own troops and sabotage would be of particular help to Allied assault troops on the beaches. Furthermore, by capturing agents, especially those in radio contact with Britain, they hoped to gain more definite information as to where the main thrust of the invasion would be made. Hence their increased activity and heightened level of alert.

More trained security police were drafted into the south-west area of France and they employed new investigative techniques. At times, for example, they would descend swiftly upon a farmhouse where they believed agents could be hiding and then they would just sit still, silent, smoking. And more to the point, listening.

It was with exactly such a ploy that British SOE agent Yvonne Baseden was captured. Yvonne had joined the WAAF aged eighteen, became the youngest officer ever to be posted to Intelligence duties and then joined SOE, eventually parachuting into France to start a new group of the underground army. By day she carried messages between groups and at night she tapped out messages to headquarters in London. In August 1944 she had been ordered by London to be at the dropping zone with sufficient men to receive the biggest arms drop ever contemplated. She was to be there twenty-four hours before the expected drop and to send messages of 'OK' every ten minutes just before the planes took off. For this was not to be the usual individual night drop: a whole flight of US Flying Fortresses were to arrive by first light.

At dawn, on a grey Sunday morning, everything had gone according to plan. Eight hundred Maquis waited until a far-off rumbling grew into a throbbing roar which shook the earth and the sky was filled with falling containers. Swiftly the Maquis swooped on them and spirited them all away. Yvonne tapped out the last 'OK' signal to London.

The next day, she, her chief, and seven sub-group leaders were sitting down to a small celebratory meal in the rambling old cheese factory which was their headquarters, when the woman who looked after them ran from the window shouting two words: 'Les Boches!' The Maquis cleared the kitchen and table and ran to their pre-arranged hiding places, under floorboards, in the loft, and among stacks of cheeses in the cellar. All was quiet when the Germans arrived. Nothing suspicious. But they sat down and waited, silent and still for well over an hour. Then it happened. A faint sound as perhaps someone eased an aching joint in a cramped space. It was enough. A thorough search began.

Two hours later they had all the men. Yvonne, wedged into a narrow gap in a log pile, heard them arrested one by one. Then a German kicked a log and saw Yvonne. He grabbed a handful of her hair and hauled her out. Then he felled her to the ground with a powerful punch to the jaw. She was thrown unconscious into the back of a truck and then began her long painful journey to Ravensbruk concentration camp.

Capture by the Gestapo or Milice was an everyday hazard which all agents had to accept. Pearl came within moments of arrest one day when she was bounding up the stairs of a three-storey apartment house to visit a contact. She stopped in full stride on hearing a loud hiss from the concierge who ran towards her whispering: 'Where are you going?' She told him. 'Quick. Come down. The Gestapo are there, waiting.'

This time their waiting game failed.

For anyone like Pearl, co-ordinating the activities of a large Resistance group and herself participating, the risks were enormous. She was aware that it was dangerous to remain too long in one location where rumour and radio direction-finding equipment might pin-point her operational base, but she accepted the risk. There was a job to be done. The main railway line between Bordeaux and Paris had to be cut and kept out of action. Her circuit, 'Wrestler' (with the neighbouring circuit, 'Shipwright'), was constantly in action on that line making, in all, more than eight hundred interdictions. No wonder the Gestapo so desperately needed to capture her that they offered a million francs for information leading to her arrest. Her picture was plastered all over the Châteauroux–Valencay–Issoudun area. But those 'Wild West' style posters did no more to restrict her activities than they did those of the villains of the badlands of the Wild West itself.

Night after night, Wrestler units went out attacking communications. And when German engineers brought in gigantic cranes to lift derailed engines back on to the line, they blew up the cranes too. They derailed trains carrying troops whether heading for action or going on leave, inflicting heavy losses on the Wehrmacht.

Another vital target for Wrestler's attention were the telephone communications concentrated on Orléans. They put the German Signals regiments there out of action completely just before D-Day and attacked them so frequently afterwards that they never got their cables working properly before the whole military garrison there moved back to Germany.

There was, however, to be a far greater task for Pearl Witherington's Wrestler. On 5 June 1944 her radio operator rushed across to her with the one message they had long been waiting for: 'Action stations!' Le Jour, J Day, had arrived. Now they were about to make their final effort. After years in which their usefulness had been doubted and funds begrudged, they were going to be put to the test. It was going to be bloody, vicious, and ultimately obscene.

They were going to take on the might of the Das Reich 22nd SS Panzer Division. This crack German division numbering 15,000 (a third of them, incidentally, French from Alsace) with 209 tanks and self-propelled guns, set out from Montauban in southern France on 8 June 1944 hoping to dash along the 450 miles north to Normandy in three to four days. Haste was imperative if they were to arrive in time to reinforce the battered German divisions opposing the Allied assault forces and lead the counter-attack which would drive the invaders back into the sea for another Dunkirk.

The Resistance groups had their orders too. Pearl Witherington lost no time in informing all her junior commanders. The Das Reich SS Panzer Division must be held up for as long as possible, *at all cost*. A formidable task for a group of enthusiastic amateur soldiers armed mainly with light weapons they had picked up when the French Army collapsed in 1940, and improvised mines and bombs. They went into the encounters with grim determination. But would the cynics who derided the efforts of SOE and Resistance groups be proved right in their belief that in the end wars were won by the big battalions and not by meddling amateurs?

The first Maquis attack upon the division was a feeble one at Cressenac on 8 June when eighteen out of the twenty-five Maquis engaged were killed. At Bretenoux, the next day, the Maquis were somewhat more effective, killing fifteen Germans and wounding thirty. The division drove on to Brive la Gaillarde with one of the Maquis corpses strapped across the bonnet of the leading armoured car. To the division now came news that the German garrison in their next town, Tulle, had fallen to the Maquis. SS Major Heinrich Wulf attacked and cleared the town with little difficulty and was going to press on northwards when an officer raced up to him saying that forty German army corpses had been found in a mutilated condition. Their testicles had been cut off and stuffed in their mouths. This final provocation brought a swift response. Reprisals were announced through a megaphone from the back of a fire engine which toured the streets ringing its bell. The message was short: for every German killed, ten Maquis would be hanged.

Executions began immediately. Every male in the town was rounded up and those who might be identifiable as Maquis were strung up immediately from street lamp-posts and telegraph poles. This 'identification' was often on the most tenuous grounds: 'You've got dirty shoes. You can't be a law-abiding citizen!'[16]

By the time that ninety-nine of those Tulle citizens were dangling from poles and posts throughout the town the divisions realized that yet again they were falling behind schedule for their journey to Normandy. The convoy re-assembled and off the SS troops moved, their nerves frayed.

Such was the mood of the Das Reich division when the forward company ran into the courageous young English girl, Violette Szabo, whose husband had lost his life at El Alamein fighting with the Free French Forces. His death had greatly affected her. At first she was stunned with grief, then gradually roused to a fury so that she cried out one day: 'I want to fight with a gun in my hand.' She joined the SOE, determined to fight the German enemy with everything she had and became the best shot of all women SOE agents.[17]

Now, with a Sten gun and eight magazines cradled in her lap she was being driven along quiet country roads near Salon-la-Tour by the local Maquis leader, Jaques Dufour (code-named Anastasie). It had been a quiet, peaceful trip. They had covered that route to Pompadour many times before and as they meandered up the small hills and down the narrow valleys in the old Citroën car, Violette and her companion had been singing choruses from their childhood songs. Then, suddenly just as they approached the first small houses of the village, Anastasie jammed on his brakes. Violette had seen the danger too, and shouted 'Germans!'

Both she and Anastasie jumped from the car and ran, bent almost double, behind a low hedge alongside the road, the way they had come. Shots rang out. German Schmeissers began spraying the hedge bottom. Together they broke cover, running full pelt zig-zag fashion up a hill towards a small copse. Bullets cracked around them. Violette fell. Not a bullet had touched her but her ankle, still weak after being injured in parachute training, had given way. Georges Guingoin told the story of how this courageous young woman was caught:

> Strenuously refusing to let her companion help – he wanted to carry her – the English girl bravely told him to save himself. With superhuman effort she held out against the pursuers, firing machine-gun bursts at them while Anastasie made a desperate run for safety. He managed to reach a small farm, owned by the Montintin family, and hid in a woodshed; three women in the family hurriedly covered him with logs and branches. They were just in time. A German half-track roared into the farmyard and soldiers jumped out shouting questions at the family. Had they seen a man running along the fields? The family feigned surprise. They had seen nothing. Neither the buildings nor the house were searched. Anastasie was safe.[18]

Violette, however, was now surrounded. Figures closed in and seized her. Soon, after months of torture and incarceration at Ravensbruk, she was to pass, in the euphemistic jargon of the SS, into the 'night and the fog'.

On 26 January 1945, at Ravensbruk concentration camp, Violette Szabo was shot.

Her colleague, Anastasie, had got clean away from the skirmish, to organize his guerilla band for further attacks on German troops, but there was a price to be paid. On Saturday 10 June 1944, a battalion of the Das Reich division drove into the nearby market town of Oradour-sur-Glane.

That morning the streets were full of people from the surrounding villages and the town of Limoges who had come to buy farm produce on the black market. In the schools, sixty boys and 106 girls were waiting, bored, in their classrooms for it was the day of the annual medical inspections. Outside, in the shops the talk was mainly about the latest big news, the Allied landings in Normandy, but even that took second place to the main task of finding the best bargains amongst those items of food which were difficult to get. In any case, the fighting was far enough away in Normandy not to cause any fear. No one

had seen many German troops about recently. Saturday
morning shopping could go on peacefully.

At 2.15 that afternoon, however, the scene in that small
market town changed abruptly. German half-tracks rattled into
the main square, helmeted infantry jumped out pointing rifles
at people and houses. Two SS troopers marched forward
beating a drum and called for the entire population to assemble
in the square. Unsuspectingly, 604 civilians were gathered.
They were told by the SS company commander, Sturmbann-
führer Dickmann, that explosives were reported to have been
hidden in the town and that a search of every house and a
check of identity cards was to be made. Under armed guards,
men were herded into barns and garages, the 400 women and
children were packed into the church. There they waited,
wondering what it was all about, and talked in whispers. A
single shot rang out from the direction of the square. At this
signal, SS guards in each building squeezed their triggers,
pouring rapid fire into the cowering groups of men, women
and children. When firing stopped, more SS soldiers heaped
straw and chairs on the bodies of the dead and dying and set
fire to the lot. Roofs collapsed on the nightmare spectacle
beneath.

Of the 652 inhabitants of that small town, 245 women, 207
children and 190 men perished. Ten survived. Though badly
burned they had simulated death and thus escaped to tell the
tale.

News spread rapidly across France but Resistance groups
were undeterred and as the Das Reich division moved on,
bearing a conspicuous array of loot, they were harassed all the
way by skirmishes with Maquisards in Pearl Witherington's
area. She was herself in the midst of the fighting. On 11 June
1944, five days now after D-Day, she and 150 French patriots
were attacked and surrounded by 2,500 German infantry. A fire
fight began which lasted fourteen hours. At one time, Pearl was
cornered by Germans and dived into a cornfield. She crawled
and lay hidden for hours in the blazing sun whilst the enemy
raked the field with fire.

'I had to be very careful how I moved,' she recalled. 'I
watched the heads of the corn above me and as they were
stirred by the breeze I moved a little closer to the edge of the
field. I had to wait until the wind moved the corn, otherwise
the Boche would have noticed it moving and fired directly at
that spot. But they finally gave up and I managed to get away.[19]

The rush to join the Maquis after D-Day had now increased dramatically and soon Pearl had a difficult job on her hands. 'It meant organizing 1,500 men into active guerilla teams within a short period of time. It was not my official mission but events got the better of me, and I had to make the best of my modest capabilities, to organize these men into a workable unit.'[20]

Modest capabilities?

By the time a French officer came to take command of Pearl's group in the middle of September 1944, she was controlling 3,500 men, who apart from the damage inflicted upon the enemy by sabotage operations, had killed 1,000 Germans in four months and had been largely responsible for forcing the surrender of a further 20,000. It was not surprising, then, that when the US Seventh Army and the First French Army, which had landed together at Toulon in August 1944, linked up with the US Third Army advancing southwards from Normandy, the disintegration of the German forces in south-west France inevitably followed.

Pearl Witherington's assignment was now complete. Her fury abated.

8

The Symbolic Heroine

Happy is your grace,
That can translate the stubbornness of fortune
Into so quiet and sweet a style.
                    William Shakespeare, *As You Like It*

At mid-day on 8 May 1945, crowds began to gather round the gates of Buckingham Palace. The Mall was black with thronging multitudes of people rejoicing at the news. The war in Europe was over. It was Victory in Europe Day.

Hundreds of thousands of people had crowded into central London. Victory crowds turned streets into playgrounds, thoroughfares were jammed with revellers; soldiers, sailors and airmen of all Allied nations mingled with civilians and towards the late afternoon thousands more were drawn down the Mall to join the vast multitude now assembled before the palace, cheering, dancing, and singing 'Rule Britannia' and 'God Save the King'. Flags, football supporters' rattles and hooters were in abundance as pent-up feelings broke loose in a carnival of rejoicing. After five years and eight long months, complete and crushing victory had crowned the Allies' unrelenting struggle against Nazi Germany. Now, as if responding to some universal instinct, the cosmopolitan crowd gathered at the hour of victory round the royal family's home and palace.

In the Bow Room there that afternoon the family was gathered too, waiting for a very important visitor. The Prime Minister, Winston Churchill, was due to arrive but packed and cheering crowds had delayed his car on its journey from Downing Street. Through the Bow Room windows now came the chant again, 'We want the King', followed by an even noisier one of 'We want the Queen'. The moment could be put off no longer. King George and Queen Elizabeth rose together and followed by the two princesses, Elizabeth and Margaret, went out on to the balcony above the great entrance to the palace.

In a great upsurge of high and rare emotion, a spontaneous cheer greeted their appearance. It was to be the first of many that evening. The next was in the company of Winston Churchill who was content to stand a little in the background while the King and Queen acknowledged the cheers, for this indeed was a royal occasion. After a few minutes of hand waving, smiling and the shedding of a few tears by the Queen, the royal party withdrew to the Bow Room again. But the crowd was not to be satisfied so easily. Their cheers grew in volume and interspersed with the cries of 'We want the King', strangely perhaps to foreigners there in the crowd, more often was the cry: '*We want the Queen*'.

At precisely nine o'clock that evening, the cheering ceased. Those thousands packed down the Mall to the palace gates stood in silence. The moment for which they had all been waiting, had arrived.

For a few brief moments hardly a sound broke the expectant hush. Then came a crackle from the loudspeakers and the unmistakable voice of the King. It came out loudly and clearly all over Britain, to his ships at sea, to his victorious troops resting in the rubble of devastated towns in Germany and Italy, to those sweating troops still battling through the swamps and jungles of South East Asia. To them all he spoke of the splendour of their achievement and of the new hope that with their victory now dawned.

Immediately after the broadcast the cry again went up, calling for the Queen. The family once again trooped out on to the balcony; the Princess Elizabeth in her uniform of ATS subaltern, Queen Elizabeth on the right of King George and Princess Margaret on his left. Together the family had stayed in a London deluged by bombs: high explosives, incendiaries, flying bombs and V2 rocket bombs. Together with Londoners they had endured hardships and dangers which sometimes seemed insurmountable. Together now they acknowledged their victory over those odds. As they left the balcony the Queen's eyes were moist with tears. The calls from the crowd had touched her. It was clear that she had carved herself a special place in the hearts and minds of all those gathered below and of the whole nation too.

During those five years and eight months of war she had

developed an indefinable aura of magic that the public responded to; they saw her as a revered mother figure who had refused to leave the hazards of London with her two daughters for the safety of Canada, though pressed by political advisers. Her reply to those suggestions had always been the same: 'The princesses cannot go without me. I cannot go without the King. The King will never go.' And so she had stayed, epitomizing all those civilian women – unlike many of the royal family, she never wore a uniform – who had carried on in the spirit of 'business as usual', even after the worst of the bombing raids. Her warming presence had given Londoners the necessary lift to help them bear the brunt of some of the worst bombing ever endured by a city. She had given of her time and of herself unstintingly. And for this she was loved. But few in that hundred-thousand crowd packed by the gates that day would know that this regal woman who, in July 1939 had been photographed by Cecil Beaton as a 'heroine of Victorian romance', was now in fact a heroine in her own right.

There was much more to her decision to stay in London than might have been indicated by the glib response to politicians and journalists who asked why she, as a mother, would not take her daughters away to a safer place than bomb-battered London. There were reasons which angered Hitler intensely. Reasons that few people knew about then and indeed of which few people are aware to this day. Reasons in keeping with the character of that remarkable Queen who warded off threats and attacks from many sides and stabilized the monarchy which, in one twelve-month period just three years before the outbreak of war, had three successive kings upon its throne.

Lady Elizabeth Bowes-Lyon had never really wanted to become involved with all the trappings, duties and public exposure which went with royalty. Twice she had declined the Duke of York's marriage proposal for that very reason, feeling such a union would restrict her freedom. But Prince Albert, the Duke of York, was persistent. He had fallen head over heels in love with this canny nineteen-year-old Scot when they first met at a friend's party in 1920. It mattered not to him that she was born a 'commoner', and that she came from an ancient Scottish family with a history as dramatic as anything in the background of the English throne. (Her father was the 14th Earl of Strathmore, one of her ancestors was Robert the Bruce, as was the awesome revolutionary Welsh warrior, Owen

Glendower, and legend even has it that one of her ancestors was burnt as a witch!) Intent however, on having the pretty Elizabeth for his bride, Albert pursued her relentlessly. Eventually his determination was rewarded; Elizabeth accepted his proposal and they were married on 26 April 1923.

The marriage was an instant success and, characteristically, having accepted her new role, Elizabeth launched into her round of duties with enthusiasm and genuine concern. She had two children, Elizabeth, born on 21 April 1926, and Margaret, born on 21 August 1930. And for those first dozen years their quietly organized married life seemed perfect. Then, suddenly their bliss was blighted by the romantic liaison of Elizabeth's brother-in-law, King Edward VIII, with an American divorcee, Mrs Wallis Simpson. Despite opposition from his family and the British Cabinet, Edward was determined to marry 'the woman I love'. He abdicated the throne, thus pitching Albert and Elizabeth into a situation neither of them had ever wanted. The significance of what had happened came as an appalling shock to Elizabeth because of her husband's utter dismay at taking his brother's place. As he ruefully remarked later to War Minister Hoare-Belisha, 'All my ancestors who succeeded to the throne did so only after their predecessors had died. Mine is still alive – very much so.'

The new King, who had never been prepared for such an elevated role, could see real problems ahead. And there were. But, fortunately he had by his side a resolute young warrior determined to ward off from her King whatever attacks might come. They were to come from all sides. Her success at handling them surely demanded the courage and resolution of a real heroine.

The first threat came from the family; from her brother-in-law, Edward and his bride, Wallis, whom she found quite alien to her own way of thinking. Elizabeth saw her as a threat not only to her own peace of mind but also to the stability of the monarchy. Wallis was furious that she was not accorded the title of 'Her Royal Highness' as were all the wives of Edward's brothers and she dearly would have loved to become the Queen consort of King Edward, if only he could regain the crown.

That possibility was being worked on shortly after the war began in earnest in May 1940. Edward at that time was acting as liaison officer with the rank of major-general to the British

Expeditionary Force in France. Then, on 16 May, six days before Hitler launched his blitzkrieg against Holland, he deserted his post, dashed home to Paris, picked up his wife and drove down to Biarritz to house her in the grand Hôtel du Palais. Two days later he returned to his post, reported to his commander-in-chief, Lord Gort, who formally gave him a reprimand and, at the same time, permission to take up a new position as British liaison officer to the French Army in the south.

Thus it happened that whilst the British Army was being shuttled off the beaches of Dunkirk the Duke and Duchess were driving along packed roads in the south of France towards Spain. Forcing his way through road-blocks, the Duke was shouting: *'Je suis le Prince de Galles. Laissez-moi passer, s'il vous plaît.'*[1]

By midnight on 20 June 1940 the Windsors were in neutral Spain. One can imagine Churchill's consternation. There, in a neutral dictatorship friendly to Germany, was a British major-general, a former King who could now quite legally be interned for the duration of the war. But what troubled Churchill more than this fate for Edward was the political manoeuvring now going on behind the scenes and the possibility that Edward himself could soon be playing a prominent part in it all. Already attempts were being made to destabilize the British government and the monarchy.

Hitler always dreamed of a 'bloodless victory' over Britain and although he planned, in a curiously inattentive though bombastic way, for an invasion of Britain, he never ceased to hope for a capitulation, to hope in fact that Britain, once isolated from all her defeated allies on the Continent, would see reason and, like the French under Marshal Petain, realize that there could be no possibility of Germany being defeated and therefore accept Hitler's peace overtures. All that was needed, he thought, was a British Marshal Petain. And what better representative could there be for that role than the man who at that very moment was openly declaring in Spain that the war with Germany was futile and that 'the most important thing now to be done was to end the war before thousands more were killed or maimed to save the faces of a few politicians.'[2]

Churchill and the Secret Service were aware of the possibilities facing Edward. They feared what might happen. It did.

The German Foreign Minister put forward a proposition on the lines that only Churchill and his clique stood in the way of Britain making peace with Germany and that it would be a good thing if the Duke would hold himself in readiness for further developments. He indicated that 'Germany would be prepared to accommodate any desire expressed by the Duke, especially with a view to the assumption of the English throne.'[3]

Whilst all these negotiations behind the scenes were going on it was clearly most important that the monarchy in Britain was seen to be firmly established. The King and his Queen had to be on show, confident and caring, reassuring civilians and servicemen and women. Consequently the royal couple travelled ceaselessly, halting their train for the night in some quiet railway siding from which they could take a stroll after dinner, undisturbed by crowds, to refresh themselves for another physically exhausting programme the next day.

They visited red-cheeked land army girls on farms, pale-faced workers in munitions factories working on shifts all round the clock to produce arms and ammunition to replace the equipment lost by the British Expeditionary Force in France; they talked to the dispirited soldiers back from Dunkirk, chatted to the garrulous enthusiasts of the new army that had so recently sprung up – the Local Defence Volunteers, without uniforms and almost without weapons but resolute in defiance. And with them the Queen even learnt to use a rifle and revolver, for in those days of parachute descents no one could feel secure against the unexpected possibility of being confronted by German assault troops. And the royal couple were prime targets. There was no remission from their round of public duties. It took courage and physical endurance to keep up those visits and constant public exposure.

All the while the King and Queen kept closely in touch with the government and secretaries in Buckingham Palace through the national telephone system connected up to the royal train. And the news they received about the Windsors then was most disturbing.

Through the Secret Service, the government knew that Edward was already discussing propositions submitted by the German Foreign Minister, Ribbentrop. They feared that he might be attracted by such a bribe as a *coup d'état* by British 'appeasers' supported by the German Foreign Office that would make Edward King again and Wallis his Queen. They believed that if both the monarchy and the government toppled then a puppet government could quite easily stage show trials like those put on by Stalin in the mid-thirties. Trials in which, perhaps, 'warmongers' such as Churchill and his cohorts would be in the dock together with all the rest of the strange collection of people named on Hitler's black list. High on that list somewhere close to the Chief of the Boy Scouts, Baden-Powell, was Elizabeth's name. It was invasion time. She could have gone to a safe place on the pretext of looking after her children but she chose to do what the nation would have expected her to do. She stayed. She stuck it out with all the others despite the fact that Hitler had already declared her to be 'the most dangerous woman in Europe' – dangerous, that is, to his own cause. Even the German ambassador in Madrid had singled her out for special mention – 'the shrewd Queen who was intriguing skilfully against the Duke and particularly the Duchess'.[4]

Meanwhile, the Windsors had moved on to Lisbon, the spy-infested capital of Portugal where Gestapo-trained secret police moved everywhere and greatly hampered the British Secret Intelligence Service so that it was difficult for Churchill to find out exactly what was happening. He suspected the worst and came to a decision. The Duke and Duchess should leave the Continent as soon as possible, even if they had to be removed by force. In a message to the heads of the Commonwealth governments and to US President Roosevelt, Churchill made his position quite clear: 'The activities of the Duke of Windsor on the Continent in recent months,' he stated, 'have been causing HM and myself grave uneasiness as his inclinations are well known to be pro-Nazi and he may become a centre of intrigue. We regard it as a real danger that he should move freely on the Continent.'[5]

He decided to offer the Duke the governorship of the Bahamas and after several weeks of prevarication the Duke and Duchess finally sailed in the first week of August 1940. The German plot had failed.

By this time, though, Hitler had at last realized that the British would not capitulate. He no longer sought a British Petain, nor a King or Gauleiter, for the long struggle to conquer Britain by force had begun. Now Elizabeth would have to show her mettle in quite another way.

At 8.32 p.m. on 7 September 1940 the most savage blow so far to fall in the battle for Britain descended upon London. After a heavy daylight raid of hundreds of planes which broke through the city's defences, the mightiest aerial assault raged on through the night amid the fire-reddened skies as wave after wave of bombers dropped thousands of high-explosive and incendiary bombs on the heart of the city and the East End. People whispered about a frighteningly big bomb the Luftwaffe was dropping too. They called it a 'land mine', though actually it was a sea mine, eight feet long, which fell silently suspended on a silk parachute and was packed with 2,200 tons of dynamite. The combined effect was that whole areas north and south of the Thames – Millwall, East India Docks, Silvertown – were flattened and set on fire. Headlines in American newspapers the next day read: 'LONDON A SEA OF FLAME'.

'Never in her long annals has the city of London been called upon to face an ordeal so cruel and so searching,' said the Lord Mayor of London in a broadcast to America. He never imagined when he spoke that the ordeal would go on continuously for fifty-seven nights from that 7 September to 3 November, as the German Luftwaffe attempted to achieve its main objectives of rendering completely uninhabitable the world's largest city and breaking the spirit of the people.

Even after the first three days, Edward Murrow of CBS Radio News was saying to his listeners across the Atlantic: 'We are told that the Germans believe Londoners, after a while, will rise up and demand a new government, one that will make peace with Germany.' He poured scorn on that idea, as did Helen Kirkpatrick of *Chicago Daily News* on 9 September, reporting that: 'It is pretty incredible to find people relatively unshaken after the terrific experience. There is some terror, but nothing on the scale to make Britons contemplate for a moment anything but fighting on. Fright becomes so mingled with a deep, almost uncontrollable anger that it is hard to know when one stops and the other begins.'

A pertinent observation. Anger, fury, hatred, feature prominently, as we have seen already, in the motivation of heroines determined to carry on with their tasks despite fearful hazards.

It was the same story with SOE agents as with shopgirls. Fear and fury bound people together in their common contempt of danger. Mollie Panter-Downes expressed similar thoughts in her report for the *New Yorker* of those terrible fifty-seven nights of continuous bombardment when an average of two hundred bombers attacked London every night:

The Blitzkrieg continued to be directed against such military objectives as the tired shopgirl, the red-eyed clerk, and the thousands of dazed and weary families patiently trundling their few belongings in perambulators away from the wreckage of their homes. After a few of these nights, sleep of a kind comes from complete exhaustion. The amazing part of it is the cheerfulness and fortitude with which ordinary individuals are doing their job under nerve-wracking conditions. Girls who have taken twice the usual time to get to work look worn when they arrive, but their faces are nicely made up and they bring you a cup of tea or sell you a hat as chirpily as ever. Little shopkeepers whose windows have been blown out paste up 'Business as usual' stickers and exchange cracks with their customers.[6]

The Queen saw it as her paramount duty to be among these young heroines and all of those who had had their homes wrecked and loved ones killed or maimed. She drove with the King through rubble-blocked streets, stopping to talk to dull-eyed, empty-faced women, many of them carrying cheap little cardboard cases and bulging shopping bags containing all they could salvage. The royal couple brought smiles to the faces of men in flat caps, with collarless shirts and white scarves round their necks, and the Queen braced herself against the all-pervading acrid stench of cordite from high-explosive bombs, leaking gas, charred wood, smouldering rubber, fractured sewers and drains, and pulverized plaster.

Worse than all that however, she had to brace herself against the sights of mutilated bodies, women and children, being pulled out of the wreckage: sights which made even hardened war correspondents sick.

Day after day they faced this stress. The Queen always supported her husband, helping him to overcome his pronounced stutter, more often than not speaking for him,[7] showing that they were with the bereaved in sympathy, reassuring them and giving them strength. Even today, Bill Bartley remembers the lift that those few words by the Queen gave them all. He told her so fifty years later when she revisited the Hallsville School at Canning Town, where in 1940 seventy people who were using the school as a rest centre were killed. 'Everyone was downhearted after that raid but then the King and Queen came. She picked her way over the rubble ignoring signs of unexploded bombs and put her arms round people covered in blood and dirt, consoling them. Somehow it gave us all strength.'

But not everybody in the East End was of the same mind as Bill Bartley, as yet another threat to the Queen's position emerged, from an unexpected quarter. Discontent was being stirred up by the Communists claiming that whilst the working class, who were bearing the brunt of the air raids, had to make do with the squalor of inadequate air-raid shelters and the railway arches of Hungerford Bridge, the rich had lush provision, having access to the deep shelters of the Café de Paris,[8] the Hungarian Restaurant, the Dorchester and Savoy hotels. Agitators for the Communist Party put round the idea that once again it was the under-privileged who were having to suffer the worst of this capitalist war.

To be fair, it did indeed seem to be the case that the East End was the main target for all the raids and this, in fact, brought forth a comment from the commander-in-chief of the country's anti-aircraft defences, General Pile, appearing to support the Communists' point of view. He said: 'It seemed as if the Germans thought that by concentrating on this part of London with its large alien population it would cause such consternation as seriously to endanger the government's position if not to force them to make peace.' And Harold Nicholson noted on 17 September: 'Everybody is worried about the feelings in the East End, it is said that even the King and Queen were booed the other day when they visited the destroyed area.'[9]

A Communist MP, Phil Piratin, resolved to make the most of this situation in his attack on the established order. On 15 September, as soon as the sirens sounded, he roused a hundred people to action and led them to the Savoy – the nearest hotel to the East End – and demanded access to the Savoy's deep shelter. By law the demonstrators had to be allowed in, but unexpectedly the 'All Clear' blared forth fifteen minutes later and to the great relief of the Savoy staff and guests, the demonstrators had no choice but to leave. As these Communist demonstrators filed out, however, they had a quick 'whip round' for the head porter and filled his hands with coppers. Further credibility in Communist propaganda about air raids being directed merely on the homes of the workers evaporated completely when news leaked out that the royal home itself, Buckingham Palace, that week had been singled out for special attention by a Luftwaffe bomber.

It was a cloudy day with very heavy rain and the royal

couple had just returned from Windsor. They had gone upstairs to rest when the air-raid siren sounded. Through the open windows they could hear the distinctive throbbing rumble of a German bomber. A Heinkel was circling the city as if looking for its target.

At the RAF station at Kenley, thirteen miles south of London, the operations room received an urgent call from its group headquarters. It caused them to telephone the crew room with an unusual request. The weather had clamped down, visibility was exceptionally poor, nevertheless they asked for a volunteer to take off and look for a German Heinkel bomber which was somewhere over London. 'But,' they warned, 'owing to unbroken cloud everywhere in the south-east, whoever goes up will probably be unable to land. It will mean baling out.'

A shy, young Yorkshireman, the dare-devil Sergeant Ginger Lacey, heard the call and as he had often wondered what it was like to bale out, agreed to take off and stalk the Heinkel.

Flying at 14,000 feet, above the thick layer of clouds and guided by the controller, he turned south, then to the east, next to the south-east and back to the east again without seeing anything of the Heinkel.

The King and Queen had seen it though. It came screaming out of low cloud straight down the line of trees along the Mall, dropping its bombs on the palace. The King pulled his wife to the floor, where they lay with debris falling around them. He recalled the scene vividly:

> We saw the bombs falling by the side of the Palace into the Quadrangle. We saw the flashes and heard the detonation as they burst about eighty yards away from us. The blast blew in the windows opposite to us and two great craters appeared in the Quadrangle. From one of these craters water from a burst water main was pouring out and flowing into the passage through the broken windows.[10]

Six bombs had fallen close to where the King and Queen had been resting in the small sitting room, two in the Forecourt, two in the quadrangle, one on the chapel wrecking it completely, and one in the garden. Before the last of the masonry had finished toppling, the intruder had zoomed off into the clouds again. But not to disappear.

Sergeant Ginger Lacey had been guided all too accurately by his controller for that. He was in the right spot in that cloudy sky just at the moment the Heinkel appeared.[11] 'I saw it slipping through the cloud tops, half in and half out of cloud, making for the coast. I didn't know where I was, because I hadn't seen the ground since taking off. I dived down on him and got in one quick burst which killed his rear gunner.'

At this the Heinkel dived into the cloud as Lacey, coming close behind him, throttled back and dropped on to his tail. Through the side quarter windscreen panel of his Hurricane, Lacey could still see the Heinkel and kept close enough in all the Heinkel's evasive turns. Eventually, thinking he had lost the shadowing fighter, the German pilot broke cloud just as Lacey was dropping into a position from which he could open fire. By this time though, the dead German gunner had been pulled away from the rear turret and Lacey received a burst of German machine-gun fire which made a gaping hole in the bottom of his cockpit. He put his finger on the trigger of his own guns and kept it there until they all stopped firing. By this time both the plane and his clothing were on fire. The Heinkel was now diving steeply through the clouds. Lacey baled out, still burning. As he neared the ground, to his horror he found himself gazing straight down the barrels of a home guard's shotgun. He swore as loudly as possible, using 'a lot of Anglo-Saxon words' and a few more recent curses. The home guard lowered his gun. 'Anyone who can swear like that couldn't possibly be a German,' he said.[12]

The Heinkel crashed on Victoria Station.

There was a sequel to that bombing of the palace which is worth a digression to relate. Six months later, when Sergeant Lacey had become Pilot Officer Lacey, he was returning from a sweep over Le Touquet, in a Spitfire this time, and was coming in to land when he noticed a group of officers standing as usual counting in the returning fighters. He thought there was something unusual about the group. Even from two hundred feet he could see everyone was in 'best blue' uniform and one figure was standing a little apart from the others. As Lacey looked a little more closely after he had landed he recognized King George. Lacey was sent for and presented to the King as the officer who had shot down the Heinkel which bombed the palace.

Whilst he was talking to His Majesty, Ginger Lacey noticed that the officers' mess bar had opened and with spontaneous politeness, he asked, 'Would you like a drink, Sir?'

The King replied, 'Yes please,' and Lacey turned to the

barman and without a second thought said, 'Two beers please'. As he handed them over, Lacey noticed a frown on the face of the commander-in-chief Fighter Command, and some apprehension too on the faces of the accompanying staff officers and station commander. The King raised his glass and downed the beer. It was only when the King had his next drink that Lacey noticed he was drinking sherry.[13]

The reaction of the King to the bombing of his palace is interesting but might seem strange today. It should be remembered that he served as a Royal Navy sub-lieutenant in the Battle of Jutland in World War I. He had seen action before and his feelings after that air raid were of tremendous exhilaration; he was actually pleased that he should be sharing the dangers of his subjects in the capital.

Naturally after this near disaster the Queen was once again urged to leave the capital for a safer place of residence. She was still adamant, however, that she would not leave. In fact the episode caused her to utter her famous comment: 'I'm glad we've been bombed. It makes me feel we can look London's East End in the face.'

Now as the Queen walked round the shattered city, heartening and consoling those who had suffered personal loss, there was no doubting the affection in which she was held. These people felt the Queen's resolution and fortitude were a perfect complement to their own.

The real test for that fortitude, though, was yet to come. It would be a long drawn-out experience that very nearly broke the morale of Londoners absolutely.

It began late in the evening of 15 June, just nine days after the Allied landings in Normandy. Captain Harry Butcher, the naval aide to Supreme Allied Commander General Eisenhower, was taking a final stroll round the estate of the headquarters close to London. He filled his lungs with the cool fresh air, deliberately ventilating them fully after a long session in the fug of the chain-smoking general's office. He cocked his head on one side to listen more carefully to the put-a-put sound of an approaching two-stroke motorcycle engine. There was something odd about the sound though. As it grew nearer he suddenly knew why. It was passing overhead. And trailing behind it was a fiery red flame!

The long-feared, much discussed, unmanned missile had arrived: Hitler's secret weapon – the flying bomb. Germany's

promised 'Retaliation' ('*Vergeltung*') for the terror bombing by
the RAF of their cities had begun. Within the next twenty-four
hours more than two hundred of those missiles came against
London and over three thousand in the next five weeks.

To Londoners they were known as 'doodle-bugs' or
'buzz-bombs'. They flew at speeds between 250 and 400 miles
per hour – the limit for most Allied fighters – carrying the
explosive of a 2,000 pound bomb. The weapon was guided,
approximately, on to its target by a magnetic compass and
when its propellor had revolved a pre-set number of times,
a mechanism was tripped and the engine cut.

Harry Butcher knew what to expect then and wrote in his
diary: 'They say you have two seconds to find shelter when the
hiss and put-put stops because the plane immediately dives to
the ground'.[14]

Now Londoners lived in terror. Edna Viner, a young, newly
qualified state registered nurse who had survived the
nightmare of the Coventry blitz in November 1940, was in
London for specialist training in Moorfields Eye Hospital and
she recalled the horror of those eighty days of the flying bombs
when people walked about semi-dazed from lack of sleep.
Days when nearly everyone in London was affected with the
jitters which caused them to jump whenever a door banged or
a motorcyclist approached.

> It was a regular routine for all nurses to spend the nights on
> mattresses in the basement of the hospital, sharing head to toe
> with your best friend or others. The hospital was hit several
> times. On one occasion, a heavy wooden beam fell on to my
> friend and across my legs. Other debris split and bruised my
> head. We were quickly evacuated to another hospital and I
> remember the scene vividly as I looked back through the
> ambulance doors. The nurses' home was ablaze![15]

No one was safe from such random attacks and the
government decided to give the horrific facts to the public,
thinking this course was better than secrecy which only
seemed to encourage exaggerated rumours. The chief censor's
view was that the more the truth was told the higher stood
morale.

Now it was a testing time for London's nerve. Now more
than ever the symbol of the heroic mother figure, Her Majesty
the Queen, had more to do in rallying the British public, going

into streets long before the last 'All Clear' had faded. She would pick her way through the smoking rubble of small terraced houses whilst bloody bodies of the maimed and dead were brought out from piles of bricks and charred beams.

She never felt that she was any braver than the thousands who crawled out of collapsed buildings and then turned back to help pull out those still trapped. But she was no less courageous either. She was not forced to stay in London but she stayed of her own free will, showing that she too could live up to the new motto. No longer was it 'Business as usual' but 'We can take it.'

They had a lot to take. More than 1,500 bombs reached land, killing 4,175 and seriously injuring a further 12,000 people. Three-quarters of a million houses were devastated, 23,000 beyond repair. Flying bombs had such a powerful blast and dropped with so little warning that tragic effects were inevitable. One bomb landing near Churchill's home at Westerham killed, by cruel mischance, twenty-two homeless children who had gathered together in a refuge built for them in the woods.

It was about this time too that Ernest Hemingway, perhaps the greatest American writer of his time, had arrived in London to become war correspondent for *Colliers* magazine. He was based in the Dorchester Hotel. Now aged forty-four, and with a cultivated image of a hard-drinking man of action, he was about to have genuine first-hand experience of London's ordeal of the flying bombs.

On Sunday 18 June he was drinking bourbon with Admiral Lovette, the US Navy's public relations chief and two US Special Services lieutenants, North and Burke. Some five hundred yards from the Dorchester that bright Sunday morning, the worshippers began to assemble for the morning service in the Guards' Chapel.

Those Sunday morning services at the Guards' Chapel in Wellington Barracks were usually quite fashionable occasions even in shabby, rationed London in its fifth year of the war, when clothing was on coupons and quality was restricted to 'Utility' standard. Everyone dressed for the occasion. And this morning was something extra special for the Guards Armoured Division, comprising the elite of the Guards Brigade officers. It was marshalling then in London to take part in the Battle for Normandy. There were, also as usual, plenty of Very Important People who liked to parade themselves at the Guards' Chapel in order to keep in the public eye. On this memorable occasion, the preacher was no less a personage than the Chaplain General to the Forces himself.

When the doors of the chapel closed, every seat was taken, pews were so tightly packed that arms holding hymn books were jammed close to everyone's side. The shuffling ceased and the Chaplain General rose to address the congregation; he was surprised to find that his voice had lost its usual control. Its pitch varied unaccountably when he spoke of 'our beloved chapel'. Later he confided to a friend with some awe that he had sensed 'a strange unfamiliar sadness and doom overshadowing the sacred precincts'. That, however, was later. The service proceeded following its usual routine.

Over at the Dorchester, the Hemingway assembly was well into its routine too of pre-lunch drinks and the conversation, not surprisingly, had drifted onto the topic of the V-1 bombs which were buzzing into London that very morning. The self-styled 'war veteran' Hemingway, bolstered by bourbon, was holding forth and putting on a bold front, expounding his pet theory that no one should feel fearful or in danger unless being shot at personally. It was at this precise moment that the bored Special Services officer, Lieutenant North, who knew more about fear than Hemingway ever would, was gazing out of the open window and remarked with concern in his voice that the infernal German missiles now seemed to be heading directly towards the Dorchester.

He was not far out. The buzz-bomb that caught his eye cut its engine some four hundred yards away, hovered momentarily and then headed straight for the packed Guards' Chapel. There they were then, standing shoulder to shoulder, lustily singing 'All the earth doth worship Thee'. That much, ATS Subaltern Sheppard-Jones well remembered. She had not heard the engine of the approaching bomb. 'There was a noise so loud it was as if all the waters and the winds in the world had come together in mighty conflict and the Guards' Chapel collapsed upon us in a bellow of bricks and mortar ... One moment I was singing the Te Deum and the next I lay in dust and blackness, aware of one thing only – that I had to go on breathing.'[16]

Buddy North, in the Dorchester, saw the buzz-bomb crash to earth and he, with his fellow officer, ran through the streets to see how they could help. Their services were badly needed for 119 men and women, mainly in the Armed Forces, had been killed outright and 102 seriously injured, with another 32 slightly hurt.

Lying trapped among the debris of the fallen masonry was ATS Subaltern Sheppard-Jones. She heard 'screaming, screaming, screaming like an animal caught in a trap … My eyes rested with horror on a blood-stained body … the body of a young soldier whose eyes turned unseeingly to the sky … I tried to convince myself that this was truly a nightmare, one from which I was bound to wake up.' But it was not. The young woman officer was disabled for life. 'I still felt no pain but I did begin to have an inkling that I was badly injured. I turned my head towards a guardsman who was helping with the rescue work and hysterically cried: "How do I look? Tell me, how do I look?" The guardsman replied, "Wonderful, Madam. You look wonderful to me!"'

Some hours later, after Miss Sheppard-Jones had been moved to St Mary's Hospital, she learnt the truth of her condition. 'My spine was fractured and my spinal column damaged … I was paralysed from the waist downwards.' Miss Sheppard-Jones joined the thousands who were to be maimed for life by this new weapon.

These frightening V-1 raids continued for over two months. On one occasion a total of 200 flying bombs fell on London within twenty-four hours. Now the nerves of all Londoners were on edge. Joan Bright Astley, who then organized a confidential service of information to the commanders in the field, recalled:

> I can say for myself that I was always listening; in the street I wished the traffic would stop, among my friends that they would not talk, because there might be a flying bomb approaching. When I did hear the jumping, throbbing, mechanical noise echo through the sky, my heart missed a beat, I waited alert, to see if it passed over, or if the engine cut out, ready to crouch under a desk or table away from windows. A sickening moment of suspense, then 'Crrrrmp' and silence again.[17]

To view the terrible effects of those raids, day after day, was a debilitating, stressful experience in the extreme but the Queen never faltered in her round of visits to the most recently bombed areas. In some way her actions resembled those of an old-time monarch, in the thick of the battle leading his countrymen.

Worse times were to come.

On 8 September 1944 the first giant long-range rocket landed in Chiswick. Churchill's immediate reaction was to censor all comment. No public announcement was to be made. This new weapon now made obsolete every other form of war weapon. It was a terrifying device, a fifty foot long, ten-ton missile carrying 12,000 pounds of high explosive, which flashed through the sky at supersonic speed. There was no sound, no warning. The first indication was a devastating explosion which could be heard ten miles away.

A reporter who asked if the massive crater at Chiswick could have been made by a new type of bomb was told: 'It might have been a gas main.'

Yet again it was the poorest districts of London that suffered most. Some idea of the carnage can be gleaned from individual accounts. Peter Davis was just coming home from work one evening at six o'clock, to his house in Shardeloes Road, Deptford. 'One minute it was normal rush hour with people scurrying across the street and then the whole road erupted into flame, dust, smoke and debris. For a hundred yards houses were battered down. They said, when casualties were finally counted, there were thirty dead and nearly two hundred badly injured.'

By 10 November 1945 the truth had to be told. Churchill announced to the House of Commons that the enemy had been using a long-range rocket and that no mention had hitherto been made for fear of helping the enemy.

Rockets continued to rain down upon the capital with what seemed to be ever-increasing intensity for seven long months until the Allied armies finally broke through the defences of the Siegfried Line, crossed the Rhine and were thrusting deep into the Reich with little resistance.

But, on the evening of 28 March 1945, all that was just another of those war communiqués on the six o'clock news. What mattered more to London mothers was the other news that made the day so memorable. No rockets had fallen that day. The terror was over. Tomorrow their children could play out on the pavements beneath the trees without the threat of death suddenly striking from the skies.

The war was virtually over too for Queen Elizabeth. She had stayed with her people for five and a half years of unprecedented peril. It had taken guts and a steady nerve. Buckingham Palace itself had been hit by bombs and rockets nine times and both she and the King had several narrow escapes, never made public until well after the war.

She too had known personal loss and anxieties; King George's brother, the Duke of Kent, was killed flying on active service in the summer of 1942 and her cousin, Viscount Lascelles, in the Grenadier Guards, was wounded and captured on the Italian front. These sorrows were never paraded but had all taken their toll.

By the time Germany surrendered unconditionally on 7 May 1945 and the war in Europe ended, the Queen was very worried about her husband's health. He was drained, mentally and physically exhausted. And he never really regained the buoyant good health of his pre-war years. Within seven years her beloved 'Bertie' was dead. Now, 'that most valiant woman' as Churchill described her, bore her grievous loss with the same control and courage she had displayed to bombed-out East Enders. Now her daughter was Queen and she had to get on with her life alone. Alone like so many widows and mothers at that time, who struggled to make a new life for themselves in the drab austerity of the post-war world.

9

What Happened to Them All?

For centuries women have sought to take hold of life and change it, to free themselves from a world in which men saw themselves as 'top dogs', filling some Stone Age role of hunter, fighter, and protector; a world in which women were excluded from many social and occupational spheres.

When the Second World War broke out, thousands of women seized the opportunities it afforded to liberate themselves from the confines of the domestic role and tackle tasks once considered too technical or hazardous. They took on responsibilities which gave them a fresh identity and an understandable motive for rejecting hearth and home. Quickly and convincingly they demonstrated their adaptability, their courage and determination not merely to cope with complicated and dangerous situations encountered on active service but to excel in them. In fact, they proved beyond any debate whatsoever, that when the crunch comes, men and women are very much alike with similar capabilities, skills and emotions.

What was not so easy for them was the return, once the war ended, to their pre-war positions in society. Many never altogether re-adjusted. They were left with a profound nostalgia for a lost sense of comradeship and the thrill of living dangerously. Many, too, found their awareness of female oppression heightened once their military status was taken away from them. Others, though, yet again demonstrated their innate ability to cram many lives into one lifetime.

Readers might like to discover what happened to the heroines featured in this book and the sequels to their experiences. Their stories are given in alphabetical order for ease of reference.

Cardwell, Eveline
The presentation of the British Empire Medal by their Majesties King George VI and Queen Elizabeth in front of the Marine Hotel, Hornsea, was not the end of the ordeals still to be faced by this retiring and modest farmer's wife. She was Yorkshire's choice to present a flag of the US Warship, *Bonhomme Richard*, which sank a British man o' war off Bridlington during the American War of Independence, to US Admiral H.R. Stark, Commander of the US Naval Forces, Europe, at a grand civil ceremony at Claridges Hotel attended by the US Ambassador to Britain, Admiral Pound of the Royal Navy, and a long list of other dignitaries.

Eveline was far more at home on the farm.

She did have her moments of great excitement, however, in riding side saddle with the Holderness Hunt for a further eighteen years and in training race horses. One of these, Speedy Procedure, is remembered in the Cardwell living room today by a set of shoes he wore at Beverley and Carlisle race courses where he won three times and was placed twice.

Eveline and her husband, Norman, farmed at Aldbrough, East Carlton, for a total of fifty-eight years. Norman gathered in his last harvest when aged eighty-eight (having broken both legs when he was eighty) and Eveline carried on until she died in February 1989, aged ninety-six.

They do breed them tough in Yorkshire.

Nurses of the Coventry and Warwickshire Hospital
Patients and nurses who survived the raid of April 1941 which devastated the hospital, were hurriedly evacuated to Keresley and other hospitals in the county. A skeleton staff was left to deal with any further casualties. Such was the haste of the evacuation process that for over a week the hospital administration did not know the fate of many of the patients until they were reported elsewhere. Relatives who telephoned for news were left waiting anxiously until patients were located.

Gladys Crichton, then Spencer, recalled: 'I can still see the tears of joy when relatives found their loved ones still alive.' Gladys had the pleasure of shaking hands with the then Queen Elizabeth, now the Queen Mother, when she visited Coventry in 1942.

A short time after the April raid, George Medals were awarded to Matron J.E. Burton, Sister Emma Horne (both now dead) and Hospital Governor Mr Cecil Hill, in recognition of the valour of all nursing and administrative staff. A further George Medal was awarded to another probationer nurse of the hospital, Marjorie E. Perkins, for her devotion to duty whilst employed in the surgery of a neighbouring factory. Altogether fourteen nurses throughout the country earned George Medals in those hectic months of 1940–1 when the Luftwaffe attacked London and the provinces in force.

Fifty years later, the Queen Mother paid tribute to them all during her visit to Coventry Cathedral in November 1990, to mark the fiftieth anniversary of the raids. Seven of the nurses who helped to form the original guard of honour for her visit in 1942 were there to welcome her.

Many of those nurses who endured the horror and enjoyed the comradeship of those far off days still meet regularly at reunions organized by that once probationer nurse, Edna Vine. The old saying that old soldiers never die, they only fade away is still far from the truth as far as these ladies are concerned. Mentally, if not physically, they are still as sprightly as ever.

Phillips, Claire
After her harrowing ordeal in the Philippines, Mrs Claire Phillips returned to her home town of Portland, Oregon, USA with her daughter, Dian, then seven years old.

In Portland, Claire gradually recovered her strength though she was, perhaps, never quite as healthy as before. Once the press heard about her activities as the 'American Mata Hari of the South Pacific', her story was covered by the *American Mercury* and condensed in the *Reader's Digest* magazine.

Claire then received many requests from organizers of lecture circuits for her to speak at their social functions. As a result of all this interest Claire then settled down to write her story with the assistance of Myron B. Goldsmith and it was published in 1947 by Binfords and Mort. Claire dedicated the book to the memory of her husband and the brave men of Bataan.

In recognition of her work against the Japanese in the Philippines she received a citation for valour from US General MacArthur.

Claire died in 1968.

Rowden, Diana
The postscript to the Diana Rowden story was written in a

dingy, ill-lit military courtroom in Wuppertal, North Rhine-Westphalia in 1946 when Diana's executioners were brought to trial. Ironically, it was the last desperate action of one of the four women being thrust into the cremation oven at Natzweiler that brought one of the murderers to court. The livid scars which her fingernails had etched on the cheek of her executioner, Peter Straub, were still inflamed round the edges in September 1946 when Company Sergeant Major Fred Rhodes of an SAS investigation team went to a Mannheim apartment to identify and arrest Straub.

While this chapter was being written in 1990, Fred Rhodes, then a bowling-green keeper in Doncaster, died. He had often said how the memory of those horrible scars and the terrible message they carried from the brave, dead woman had stuck indelibly in his mind for more than forty years.

Whilst Peter Straub was being tried by British military court martial, his assistant declared on oath that one of the women was still alive when Straub pushed her into the furnace.

Peter Straub was hanged on 11 October 1946, Fritz Hartjenstein, the camp commandant, was sentenced to life imprisonment but died of an illness in October 1954, the camp medical officer, Dr Rohde, and another camp guard, Berg, were hanged on the same day as Straub.

Thus the horrific story was complete. But yet not quite, for it still lingers in the minds of survivors of that Natzweiler camp. The nightmarish quality of that memory is illustrated vividly by an incident in Brian Stonehouse's life which occurred some time after he returned from the camp. It is related in Professor M.R.D. Foot's book, the official history of the SOE in France.[1] He tells how, when the gaunt-looking Stonehouse met two former friends, who were in the FANY, they hardly recognized him. They invited him to their flat for lunch for he looked so emaciated. Generously they spent the whole of their combined meat ration on him for one meal. But as the chops began to cook, Brian Stonehouse rushed out of the house and into the street with a cry of, 'I can't stand the smell of burning flesh!'

By this time, in the autumn of 1946, the Special Operations Executive, in which 3,200 women served with over a third of them on active service in various parts of the world, was being hastily wound up, leaving a dubious reputation for the way it had treated those who had given so much. Without a word, SOE abandoned the French people who had fought so gallantly in British Resistance groups and gave scant recognition to all those heroines like Diana Rowden who fought with such strength and courage. The relatives of those who died were shabbily treated too in that little information was given to them. As Vera Atkins, who helped to despatch so many agents, commented so bitterly: 'We do less than any other nation to commemorate our people.'

However, for those who can find time to go to a quiet corner of London's Wilton Place, not far from the bustle of Knightsbridge, there can be found a church which carries on its outer wall a small tablet bearing the names of women SOE agents who died for their country. They were, like Diana Rowden, dedicated but unsung heroines, for the most part forgotten by the government that came in with the peace for which they had fought. But in the minds of those who know what these women achieved, their indomitable spirit will live, burning like a bright flame in the memory.

Stavridi, Joanna

Joanna Stavridi survived the German occupation of Greece, nursing in a hospital and teaching English (the latter was forbidden by the Germans) to earn money for food which was both scarce and very expensive.

Early in the occupation, the German Command warned the Greeks that anyone detected harbouring or aiding British military personnel would be shot. This was no idle threat. Even priests were dragged from their churches, monks from their monasteries, and shot after trials which were a mockery of justice as we know it. Nevertheless, these threats did not deter Greek men and women from giving assistance to soldiers and airmen who had been left behind after the British evacuation. Help was given, generously and fearlessly.

Joanna herself hid soldiers at various times despite all the risks involved. Near Joanna's flat, as American journalist Betty Wasson reported,[2] a mother of four children was shot dead on her own doorstep by Germans who found five British soldiers in her apartment. Joanna was not to be put off even by such butchery. Once, in fact, she very nearly paid the same penalty herself. The doorbell rang late one night, German soldiers thumped noisily and impatiently on the door. Inside two British officers were hiding. They dashed silently up the stone staircase in their stockinged feet to a small box room where the family junk was stacked. They covered themselves with carpets, rugs and anything they could lay hands on. There they lay panting. Heavy boots tramped from room to room. At last a door slammed. All was quiet. Slowly they emerged.

Eventually Joanna helped these two officers to escape by sea to rejoin their units in Egypt.

When the German occupation of Greece ended Joanna was able to return to England. Her sister recalls how she looked then: 'She was in a very poor state of health owing to the privations and poor diet. Though she did not complain and said she was in good health she was in fact bloated like those starving African children seen in photographs, their bellies distended through famine.'

Joanna, though, made a good recovery, worked for many years in the United States and then returned to London. Few of her friends ever knew of her heroic exploits in Greece and Crete all those years ago for she was a very modest woman.

On 8 May 1976 she died of cancer. In her obituary in *The Times* of 12 May, film critic and author Dilys Powell wrote:

'There must still be a few one-time fighting men in Britain who will recall with gratitude the self-sacrificing devotion of the solitary nurse in the Cretan caves, those long years ago.'

Turner, Margot

On 26 September 1940, Sister Turner and several other friends from the former Japanese prison camp sailed for England and a month later landed at Liverpool. The next day they boarded a 'special' train for London. 'We soon knew', Margot Turner recalled, 'that we were back in England. That special train took eight hours for the journey to London's Euston Station!'

Sister Margot Turner spent the next six weeks of her leave with her mother at Hove, and then, putting behind her all feelings of hate and bitterness, she resumed her nursing career with the Queen Alexandra's Imperial Military Nursing Service, which, three years later, became the Queen Alexandra's Royal Army Nursing Corps.

In February 1946 Margot Turner was awarded the MBE for her wartime service and was posted to Millbank Hospital. Then began a long and distinguished period of service in hospitals all over the world as well as in the United Kingdom, culminating for her in the greatest honour of all when she was appointed Matron in Chief and Director of the Army Nursing Service. In June 1965, Brigadier Margot Turner received the highest honour of Dame of the British Empire. It was a fitting honour for such a heroine, as Brigadier Sir John Smyth, VC, MC was later to write:

'Her amazing war experiences, the endurance which had brought her through those dreadful times, and the courage that she has shown in putting them behind her, had made her a considerable heroine amongst QAs of all ranks and all ages. Many of them took her as a model and an example.'[3]

Witherington, Pearl

Months after the war in Europe was over, Pearl Witherington's gallantry over a long period as an SOE agent in France was recognized and she was recommended for the award of the Military Cross. But this, like the Victoria Cross, was a 'man's medal' for which women were not eligible. Yet Pearl, it was argued, was an exceptional case. She had done far more than many men had done for the award of the Military Cross.

Red tape, however, prevailed and some weeks later Pearl received a letter informing her that she had been awarded the MBE (Civil). She sent it back with a curt note saying that she had done nothing civil.

Nonplussed, the hierarchy sought a satisfactory solution. The Air Ministry came to the rescue and awarded her the MBE (Military Division) which went some way to recognizing the military nature of her duties. The citation recognized quite emphatically the way she had completely disregarded her own safety in leading some three thousand Maquis in the Indre region of France. A remarkable feat for a most remarkable woman.

Today no one doubts that the efforts of agents such as Pearl Witherington and the French Resistance groups helped to shorten the war. Supreme Commander of Allied Forces, General Eisenhower, said they were worth several divisions at a critical time, and that they 'played a very considerable part in our complete and final victory'.

The official historian of the SOE, Professor M.R.D. Foot, himself a former Special Air Services officer active in wartime France, summed up SOE's contribution convincingly: 'Thanks to SOE's success in raising hundreds of secret forces of lightly armed infantry scattered all over the French countryside the enemy could no longer rely on control of his own rear areas or lines of communications with his base.'

He believes that the seventeen-day delay which the Resistance groups imposed on Das Reich SS Armoured Division which had been summoned from the south of France to take part in the battle for Normandy immediately the invasion started, showed just how valuable and effective were those Resistance groups.

'All things considered,' he wrote, 'their effort was certainly worth not less than half a dozen divisions of three brigades each.'

He makes the point too that without the organization, communications material, training and leadership which the SOE had supplied, 'Resistance would have been of no military value.'

And what does Pearl Witherington herself think today?

With typical modesty, Pearl, now living in Paris, replied to my question by saying:

> I don't like talking about 'heroines'. I always say that I was parachuted in to help the Resistance. The German occupation had roused me to a fury and I wanted to hit back hard. The Resistance did their job and I did what I thought SOE would have wanted me to do when my chief was caught. I took over his job.
>
> In some ways we in SOE were looked down upon as amateurs, but no one had ever done anything like it before and we had to do everything by trial and error. We had to make decisions without reference to higher authority. This month, I had a most interesting discussion with the RAF air marshal who was responsible in 1944 for the dropping of arms and equipment to us. We talked about how we could have done it better. Just forty-five years too late.
>
> Once SOE agents and the Resistance came out into the open as fighting units it was not half so nerve-racking as the period when we were creeping about at night retrieving drops of arms, cutting railway lines and engaging in various forms of sabotage. Those were the really stressful times.
>
> As I see it now, each little pocket of resistance did its work and it was the sum of all their efforts that brought us success in a war that had to be won.

For the record, shortly before the war in Europe ended, Pearl Witherington married her childhood sweetheart and the man who had worked in the same Resistance group with her, Henri Cornioley. They have a daughter, Claire.

Pearl still enjoys living in her beloved France but makes regular visits to Britain. On the last occasion it was to address the Combined Services Staff College, Camberley.

We have, it seems, whether Pearl likes the term or not, still much to learn from heroines.

References

1 Underground Operator

1. Irene Ward in *F.A.N.Y. Invicta* (Hutchinson, 1955).

2. Interview with the writer.

3. M.R.D. Foot, *Resistance* (Eyre Methuen, 1976).

4. Serge Klarsfield, who master-minded the forcible return of the 'Butcher of Lyons' from Bolivia to face his victims, also sought to prosecute those Frenchmen who collaborated with the Gestapo and sent nearly 80,000 Jews to Auschwitz. He amassed irrefutable evidence against the Milice to use in the case against Milice Section Head, Paul Touvier, in 1990. The *Observer*, 8 April 1990.

5. Interview with the writer.

6. See William Simpson, *The Way of Recovery* (Hamish Hamilton, 1944).

7. Ibid.

8. Elizabeth Nicholas, *Death Be Not Proud* (Cresset, 1953).

9. Ibid.

10. See the obituary of B. Maurice Southgate, who worked with Jacqueline Nearne, *Daily Telegraph*, 21 March 1990.

11. Maurice Buckmaster, *They Fought Alone* (Odhams, 1958).

12. Ibid.

13. In Elizabeth Nicholas, op. cit.

14. Ibid.

15. See Anthony Kemp's *The Secret Hunters* (Michael O'Mara Books, 1986).

16. See *Natzweiler Trial*, published by William Hodge, War Crimes, Trial Series, 1949.

2 The Home Front Heroine

1. Quoted in Richard Collier, *1940 – The World in Flames* (Penguin Books, 1971). See also 'Invasion', *Daily Telegraph*, 9 July 1940.

2. Peter Fleming, *Invasion 1940* (Rupert Hart-Davis, 1957) and Charles Whiting, *Poor Bloody Infantry* (Stanley Paul, 1987).

3. Charles Whiting, op. cit.

4. Home Publicity Enquiry Minutes INF/320 PRO.

5. Ian Mclaine, *Ministry of Morale* (George Allen and Unwin, 1979).

6. Charles Whiting, op. cit.

7. As reported in the *Holderness Gazette*, 9 March 1990.

8. *Hornsea Gazette*, 9 March 1990.

9. Montgomery of Alamein, *Memoirs* (Collins, 1958).

10. See D. Collett Wadge, *Women in Uniform* (Sampson Lane, 1946).

11. On 10 July 1940 Fighter Command had 666 fighters. At the end of

September 1940 they had 665. Thus the production of aircraft had almost exactly counterbalanced the effect of the losses.

12. Norman Gelb, *Scramble, A Narrative History of the Battle of Britain* (Michael Joseph, 1980).

13. Ibid.

14. See Eric Taylor, *Women Who Went to War* (Robert Hale, 1988).

15. Norman Gelb, op. cit.

16. Interview with the writer.

17. See Eric Taylor, op. cit.

18. Citation in D. Collett Wadge, op. cit.

19. Casualties to the civilian population in Britain during the whole of the Second World War were 146,777 killed, missing, believed killed or seriously injured. This total includes 15,358 children under sixteen and 537 human beings who were never identified. Official German figures put their civilian losses at just under 3,000,000. Of these, 500,000 were killed in air raids and ground fighting; the remainder are said to have perished in the great fluxes and deportations which followed the Russian advance into Germany.

3 That Others Might Live

1. Dr Harry Winter's account 'Man in White' in *Light of Freedom* (George Allen & Unwin, 1941)

2. See Group Captain Winterbotham *Ultra Secret* (1975) and Charles Whiting, *Britain under Fire* (Century, 1986); also Altar Douglas, 'Coventry at War', *Coventry Evening Telegraph*, 1983.

3. Personal interview with the writer, and letters.

4. Cajus Becker, *Luftwaffe War Diaries* (Macdonald, 1964).

5. Personal interview in Germany, 1988.

6. Personal interview.

7. Personal interview.

8. Charles Whiting, op. cit.

9. Personal interview and account supplied by Joan Ottaway Holman.

10. Ernest Fairfax, *Calling All Arms* (Hutchinson, 1946).

11. Harry Winter, op. cit.

12. To the writer.

13. Manfred Deschner to the writer.

14. *Daily Telegraph*, Thursday 14 November 1940.

15. Ernest Fairfax, op. cit.

16. Account by Mrs Joyce Miles Testrail sent to the writer.

17. Twenty-five years later when the two met again at a reunion celebration. Report in *Coventry Evening Telegraph*, 14 November 1965.

4 Nurse Under Siege

1. I am indebted to Mr Valieri Stavridi, Mrs Margaret Stavridi and Mrs Hadjilazaro for information on this period of Joanna's life.

2. Opinion of Joanna's brother, Valieri Stavridi, in interview with the writer.

3. Said her friend, Mrs Margaret Stavridi.

4. See Compton Mackenzie, *Wings of Freedom* (Chatto and Windus, 1944).

5. Report of Colonel Hamilton-Fairley produced for the writer by Mrs Margaret Stavridi.

6. See New Zealand Nursing Service in D. Collett Wadge, *Women in Uniform* (Sampson Law, 1946).

7. Ibid.

8. Report by Colonel Hamilton-Fairley, 7 June 1941. Account from letter from Joanna to Margaret Stavridi.

9. See Charles Whiting, *Poor Bloody Infantry* (Stanley Paul, 1987).

10. Ibid.

11. Roy Farran, *Winged Dagger* (Collins, 1948).

12. In a memorandum to the Inter Allied Conference at St James's Palace, 13 January 1942.

13. In W. B. Thomas, *Dare to be Free* (Readers Union, Alan Wingate, 1953).

14. Ibid.

15. John Hetherington, *Airborne Invasion* (Angus Robinson, 1944).

16. Roy Farran, op. cit.

17. See John Hetherington, op. cit. Reports were received of a small hypodermic outfit – syringe, needles and ampoules – being found on bodies of German parachutists. British troops in North Africa were sometimes issued with benzadrine-type pills for similar reasons, as the present writer, then with the 78th Division, well remembers.

18. John Bennett, interview with the writer.

19. Charles Whiting, op. cit.

20. Roy Farran, op. cit.

21. Letter supplied by Joanna's brother, Mr Valieri Stavridi.

22. In a letter supplied by Mr Valieri Stavridi.

23. Anthony Cotterell, in *R.A.M.C.* (Hutchinson, 1945).

24. Ibid.

25. Report by Colonel Hamilton-Fairley, op. cit.

5 Survivor Against the Odds

1. Ada Harrison, *Grey and Scarlet: Letters from Army Sisters on Active Service* (Hodder & Stoughton, 1944).

2. Ibid.

3. See Margaret Kenny, *Captives* (University of Queensland Press, St Lucia, 1988).

4. Ibid.

5. Sir John Smyth, *The Will to Live* (Cassell, 1970).

6. Ibid.

7. Ibid.

8. Margaret Kenny, op. cit.

9. See also Lavinia Warner and John Sandilands, *Women beyond the Wire* (Hutchinson Arrow, 1982) and Jane Tierney *Tobo* (Judy Piatkus, 1985).

10. Sir John Smyth, op. cit.

11. Margaret Kenny, op. cit.

12. Ibid.

13. Lord Russell of Liverpool, 'The Knights of Bushido' (Cassell, 1958).

6 The Soldier's Wife Who Fought Back

1. In the foreword to Claire Phillips's book, *Manila Espionage* (Binfords and Mort, 1947).

2. Ibid.

3. Kenneth Davis, *The American Experience of War* (Secker and Warburg, 1967).

4. In Bartlett Kerr, *Surrender and Survival* (William Morrow Inc., 1985).

5. Ibid.

6. Claire Phillips, op. cit.

7. Bartlett Kerr, op. cit.

8. Claire Phillips, op. cit.

9. Heinz Höhne, *The Order of the Death's Head – The Story of Hitler's SS* (Secker and Warburg, 1969).

10. Claire Phillips, op. cit.

11. 'World War Two Investigator', No. 14, Vol. 2, No. 2.

7 Front Line Fighters

1. M.R.D. Foot, *SOE in France* (HMSO, 1966).

2. Max Hastings, *Das Reich* (Michael Joseph, 1981).

3. It was unfortunate that he did not mention the many more women of FANY who were there too.

4. In Archie Hall, *We Also Were There* (Merlin Books Ltd, 1985).

5. Irene Ward, *F.A.N.Y. Invicta* (Hutchinson, 1955).

6. Conversations between Mrs Pearl Witherington Cornioley and the writer, July 1990.

7. In conversation with the writer, July 1990.

8. Marcel Ruby, *F Section SOE* (Leo Cooper, 1988).

9. Conversation with the writer.

10. Including that of the present writer, much later.

11. Quoted from his obituary, *Daily Telegraph*, May 1990.

12. In conversations with the writer, July 1990.

13. See Irene Ward, op. cit.

14. Marcel Ruby, op. cit.

15. In M.R.D. Foot, op. cit.

16. Max Hastings, *Das Reich* (Michael Joseph, 1981).

17. R.J. Minney, *Carve Her Name with Pride* (Newnes, 1956). See also Eric Taylor, *Women Who Went to War* (Robert Hale, 1988).

18. Georges Guingoin, *Quatre Ans de Lutte sur le Sol Limousin* (Hachette, Paris, 1974).

19. See Irene Ward, op. cit. Also related personally to the writer, in July 1990.

20. In conversation with the writer, July 1990.

21. M.R.D. Foot, op. cit.

22. Ibid.

8 The Symbolic Heroine

1. See the Duchess of Windsor, *The Heart has its Reasons*, p. 335 (Michael Joseph, 1956).

2. *Foreign Relations of the United States 1940*, Vol III, 1939/4357, p. 41.

3. Frances Donaldson, *Edward VIII* (Weidenfeld and Nicholson, 1974).

4. Ibid.

5. Ibid.

6. Richard Collier, *Warcos* (Weidenfeld and Nicholson, 1989).

7. Before the Coronation a speech therapist, Lionel Logue, had been called

in to help the King speak for the formal responses of the ceremony. But it was the Queen upon whom King George depended. 'Make sure you're always where I can see you,' he insisted, and so she was, even at the height of the Blitz.

8. Ironically, the Café de Paris owner, Martin Poulsen, had fooled everybody into thinking that it had four proper floors above the dance floor. It had not. On the night of 8 March 1941, two 100 lb bombs went through the night club, killing thirty-four people – including Poulsen himself – and seriously injuring over one hundred. In the confusion that followed, looters robbed the dead and wounded.

9. Joan Bright Astley, *The Inner Circle* (Hutchinson, 1971); also Charles Whiting, *Britain under Fire* (Century, 1980).

10. To Winston Churchill in Winston S. Churchill, *Second World War*, Vol. II, (Cassell, 1949).

11. Richard Bickers, *Ginger Lacey* (Robert Hale, 1962).

12. Ibid.

13. Ibid.

14. Captain Harry Butcher, *My Three Years with Eisenhower* (Heinemann, 1946).

15. Personal interview, Edna Viner with the writer.

16. Charles Whiting, op. cit.; also Winston Churchill, op. cit.

17. Joan Bright Astley, op. cit.

9 What Happened to Them All?

1. M.R.D. Foot, *SOE 1940–46* (BBC, 1984).

2. Betty Wasson, *Miracle in Hellas* (Museum Press, 1943).

3. Sir John Smyth, *The Will to Live* (Cassell, 1970).

Bibliography

Beevor, J.G., SOE *Recollections and Reflections* (Bodley Head, 1981).

Brown, Stuart, *Forbidden Paths* (Paul Harris Publishing, 1978).

Buckmaster, Maurice, *They Fought Alone* (Odhams, 1958).

Butcher, Captain Harry, *My Three Years with Eisenhower* (Hutchinson, 1946).

Churchill, Peter, *The Spirit of the Cage* (Hodder and Stoughton, 1954).

Churchill, Winston, *The Second World War*, Vols I – VI (1949).

Cotterell, Anthony, *R.A.M.C.* (Hutchinson, 1945).

Davis, Kenneth S., *The American Experience of War* (Secker and Warburg, 1947).

Dodds, Parker, *Setting Europe Ablaze* (Springwood, 1983).

Foot, M.R.D., *Resistance* (Eyre Methuen, 1961).

———, *S.O.E.* (BBC, 1984).

———, *S.O.E. in France* (HMSO, 1966).

Ford, Corey, *Donovan O.S.S.* (Little Brown and Co., Boston, 1970).

Fuller, Jean Overton, *Born for Sacrifice* (Gollancz, 1952).

Gribble, Leonard, *On Secret Service* (Burke, 1950).

Guingoin, Georges, *Quatre Ans de Lutte sur le Sol Limousin* (Hachette, Paris, 1974).

Harrison, Ada, *Grey and Scarlet: Letters from War Areas by Army Sisters on Active Service* (Hodder and Stoughton, 1944).

Hastings, Max, *Das Reich* (Michael Joseph, 1981).

Hewison, Robert, *Under Siege* (Weidenfeld and Nicholson, 1977).

Kedward, H.R. *Resistance in France* (Oxford University Press, 1978).

Kemp, Anthony, *The Secret Hunters* (Michael O'Mara Books, 1986).

Kenny, Catherine, *Captives* (University of Queensland, 1986).

Lee, Wing Commander Asher, *Blitz on Britain* (Four Square Books, 1960).

Lucas, Celia, *Prisoners of Santo Thomas* (David and Charles, 1975).

Marshall, Bruce, *The White Rabbit* (Evans, 1952).

Maclean, Ian, *Ministry of Morale* (Allen and Unwin, 1979).

Michel, Henri, *The Shadow War* (André Deutsch, 1972).

Millar, George, *Maquis* (Chivers, 1945).

Minney, R.J. *Carve her Name with Pride* (Newnes, 1956).

Moorhead, Alan, *Mediterranean Front* (Hamish Hamilton, 1949).

Nicholas, Elizabeth, *Death Be Not Proud* (Cresset, 1953).

Pack, S.W.C., *The Battle for Crete* (Ian Allan, 1973).

Parkinson, Roger, *Attack on Pearl Harbour* (Wayland, 1973).

Popham, Hugh, *F.A.N.Y.* (Leo Cooper, 1984).

Simpson, Sqn Ldr William, *The Way to Recovery* (Hamish Hamilton, 1944).

Smith, R. Harris, *O.S.S.* (University of California Press, Los Angeles, 1972).

Ruby, Marcel, *F Section S.O.E.* (Leo Cooper, 1988).

Thomas, W.B., *Dare To Be Free* (Readers Union, 1953).

Tickell, Jerrard, *Moon Squadron* (George Mann, 1973).

————, *Odette* (Chapman and Hall, 1949).

Wadge, D. Collett, *Women in Uniform* (Sampson Low, 1946).

Ward, Irene, *F.A.N.Y. Invicta* (Hutchinson, 1955).

Warner, Philip, *The Secret Forces of World War Two* (Granada, 1985).

Wasson, Betty, *Miracle of Hellas* (Museum Press, 1943).

Whiting, Charles, *Poor Bloody Infantry* (Stanley Paul, 1987).

Index